Barbara Butler has previously written a 2,000 year history of Swilland and Witnesham in Suffolk entitled 'A Very Ordinary Place' and has contributed to various magazines.

CORRECTION:
Wooden gravel barge
ADVANCE p.170 was not
involved in this operation.

Published in 2013 by Barbara Butler
High View, Tuddenham Lane, Witnesham, IP6 9HL

© Barbara Butler 2013

The right of Barbara Butler to be identified as the author of this work has been asserted by her in accordance with the Copyright Designs and Patent Act 1998

ISBN 978-0-9926182-0-9

Printed and bound in Great Britain by:

Sharward Services Limited
Westerfield Business Centre, Main Road, Westerfield, Ipswich IP6 9AB
Website: sharward.co.uk

SAILING BARGES – THE DUNKIRK STORY

Barbara Butler

FOR Mum

also for John and all the young men who have no marked grave.

Thank you to Gary Butler, barge mate, for his relentless editing.

Front cover: Crossing with the 50th anniversary commemorative flotilla. ENA (a cross in the topsail) & CABBY, taken from PUDGE

Back cover: Skipper of PUDGE Rob Dudley & the author in Dunkirk, 1990.

CONTENTS

	Page
INTRODUCTION	4
SAILING BARGES – THE DUNKIRK STORY	5
THE GREAT WORK HORSE	9
PROGRESS AND RETREAT	16
MILITARY DISASTER	29
OPERATION DYNAMO	36
a.b. *PUDGE*, s.b. *DORIS* & a.b. *LADY ROSEBERY*	48
WAITING…..	59
THE AMAZING ARMADA	69
a.b *BEATRICE MAUD*	72
RECOLLECTIONS	77
s.b. BARBARA JEAN	86
OUR BOYS ARE COMING HOME	95
TWO TINS OF BISCUITS AND FIVE CANS OF WATER	107
WIN SOME LOSE SOME	115
THEY CAME BACK - UNBEATABLE	123
THE GLORIOUS 1st JUNE	133
ONE SMALL HOPE	145
"OPERATION COMPLETE, RETURNING TO DOVER"	163
ANOTHER 'ONE LAST STAND'	174
"WARS ARE NOT WON BY EVACUATIONS"	179
DANGEROUS WORK	187
DOVER CASTLE	192
OPERATION ARIEL	197
THE GERMANS ARE COMING	200
THE 50th ANNIVERSARY 1990	208
31st MAY 1940	227
APENDICES:	
1. TROOPS EVACUATED	229
2. ASSOCIATION OF DUNKIRK LITTLE SHIPS	230
3. French site: Epaves a Dunkerque	232
4. Essex Family History – Barges at War	234
INDEX OF BARGES MENTIONED HEREIN	235
BIBLIOGRAPHY, CONTRIBUTIONS	238
INDEX OF ILLUSTRATIONS	243

INTRODUCTION

Many of these stories are previously unrecorded accounts of the evacuation of the British Expeditionary Force during the 9 days of Operation Dynamo, May/June 1940, told by survivors and their families to Barbara Butler and friends of the Thames Sailing Barge Trust during the visit of a.b. *PUDGE* to Dunkirk in May/June 1990. At subsequent presentations more stories have emerged from the widows and children of the men who died or survived those nine days, when certain defeat was turned into a victory of courage and determination. Sadly, not all of the names of those who have spoken to us have been recorded.

The records are not complete, in that some tug-masters did not give the names of the barges they towed, or whether they stopped at Sheerness of Gravesend or, reaching the docks up-river, were towed immediately to Dover.

I have made free with the account of Operation Dynamo compiled for our trip to Dunkirk in 1990 by Simon Lavington, also Charlie Webb's account of his life, given to Richard Smith who gave it to David Wood who transcribed the work and allowed me to have a copy. Keith Webb, Charlie's son, one of the few men remaining who worked on barges in trade, has been an invaluable source. Pam Coote, Charlie's daughter also gave me some anecdotes, photographs and background of her family. I am grateful to Brian Pinner and Peter Shaw, both of whom worked to save '*ENA*'. Old friends Richard and Joan Smith permitted me to use some relevant painstaking research contained in 'The Port of Ipswich, Shipping and Trade', and 'The Thames Barge in Suffolk'. Other helpful reading material is listed later. Elizabeth Wood, past Archivist for the Thames Barge Sailing Club (now Thames Sailing Barge Trust) and her husband David are endless sources of knowledge, as are other members of the Society for Sailing Barge Research, (formerly the Society for Spritsail Barge Research) including Richard Walsh and Tony Farnham.

Sailing Barges - The Dunkirk Story

From 'THE PORT OF LONDON AUTHORITY MONTHLY, (PLA) July 1940:

"In a tribute to the Merchant Navy and other volunteers for their part in the evacuation of 335,000 Allied troops from Dunkirk, Mr. Ronald Cross, Minister of Shipping said:

'Something like a thousand small craft took part. We shall never have a complete list of all the vessels employed. Never was there a more fantastic Armada: never did a weirder collection of vessels set sail. There were pleasure steamers, cross-Channel passenger steamers, coasting craft, tugs, trawlers, drifters, motor boats and launches and motor and sailing barges. Every tug from the River Thames was taken.....'

"One day, when the earth ceases to rock from the shock of world revolution the full story of the men and craft of the Port of London that responded to the sudden emergency will be recorded., it is to be hoped by a pen worthy of the task. Now, under the existing pressure of breathtaking events it is only possible to present a disconnected story and isolated episodes of devotion and heroism.

"The Port of London Lighterage Emergency Executive undertook the task of marshalling, rationing etc., the suitable sailing barges in the port at the time. Vessels of shallow draft were preferred and their wooden construction rendered them immune from magnetic mines. Never have so many sailing barges congregated in Tilbury Docks basin. The complement of these sailing barges consisted of the normal master and crew of two and it is unquestionably invidious to distinguish between any of them in respect of the merit of their services. It is, however, permissible to record as typical the experiences of the sailing barge TOLLESBURY (R & W Paul Ltd).

"Even Thames sludge hoppers played their part. Craft less suitable for passenger transport can hardly be imagined, yet *one hopper belonging to the Tilbury Contracting and Dredging Co. succeeded in bringing off no fewer than 487 soldiers in one trip. Thousands more were taken in these little ships back to Britain. The identity of all who volunteered, and many of those whose services were utilised will never be known. They included men – and some women – from all walks of life, from the wealthy owners of motor craft to junior office clerks. They included a sailing barge hand with a wooden leg and a deck hand lad of barely 16 years".*

The following accounts are not recorded by an historian, but by a storyteller. The words of the leaders or the famous, Churchill, Ramsey, Bader and Montgomery are well recorded. But they did not lie among the dunes of Dunkirk in fear of their lives. They did not wade into the sea up to their necks, pushing aside the bodies of their comrades who had died in the water just moments ahead of them. Those are the men who talked to us, or their widows, or their sons and daughters. Those old men had often not spoken of what they had seen and suffered but in their last years wanted to tell their experiences. It is they, the privates and corporals who fight on the ground who win or lose wars for us.

The full list of vessels that took part in the evacuation of two armies from the beaches will probably never be known, whether naval or merchant ships, private or in public service. Different lists, even from reputable sources, differ in their content. Written accounts contain inaccuracies. No doubt so will this one.

Logs were lost, along with vessels and their crews. Letters home are private. The few we have must serve to describe the experiences of others. It is not surprising that in that confusion even ships logs could be less vital than the matters in hand, the urgency was to pick up stranded or drowning men. Certainly every list of spritsail barges as having participated in Operation Dynamo varies, if only by one or two craft left out or added, although it is probable that some of them registered for the operation while at

Dover or Ramsgate but were not called upon to go. A further difficulty is that although there were some 3,000 barges built, mainly during the 19th century, a few traded without being registered, especially the river barges, some owned by the London and Rochester Trading Company.

The veterans we met at Dunkirk in 1990 to a man could not tell us the name of the ship they came home on. All they could remember was their sheer exhaustion and relief at being picked up. Similarly, there were men who were prepared to die, and some who did die whose names were never recorded.

House of Commons Debrett, 12th June 1940:
Sir Henry Morris-Jones asked the Prime Minister:
> *"whether a record is being kept of the names of those who served in the evacuation of Dunkirk, apart from those in the three Services, and particularly of the men on board the small ships of our Merchant Navy; and whether it is intended that a commemorative medal, or other token of recognition, is to be given to those who took part in this episode?"*

The Lord Privy Seal Mr. Attlee:
> *"I am informed that a record has been kept of all those who were regularly entered for this operation. It has not, however, been possible to keep a complete record of the many names of those who so gallantly gave their services independently of those entered. In reply to the last part of the Question, I would refer my Hon. Friend to the answer which I gave yesterday to my Hon. Friend the Member for Stoke (Mr. E. Smith)."*

Sir H. Morris-Jones:
> *"In view of the special character of the work done by these men and of the fact that they were volunteers, in a sphere of work to which many of them were not accustomed, would my Right Hon. Friend consider issuing in the future some kind of*

recognition, either in the form of a medal or of something else?"

Mr. E. Smith:
"When considering this Question, will my Right Hon. Friend bear in mind that the men who have come home speak in the highest possible terms of the bargemen, fishermen and others who worked so strenuously, without any regard for their own lives, and who, as a result, were largely instrumental in saving many thousands of lives?"

The Dunkirk medal was finally issued in 1970.

Over 1300 vessels took part in Operation Dynamo, the official name for the Dunkirk evacuation. How many of them were Thames barges? The lists differ but certainly more than 30. Over 50 of the little ships were steam tugs. They are part of the story of our barges during May and June 1940. They served throughout at ports like Dover and Ramsgate, ceaselessly berthing and refuelling the arriving vessels and towing the little ships back and forth across the channel. Their logs are written in the words of their crew. No storyteller can equal the impact of the matter-of-fact descriptions of those nine days and nights, when the living were trying to get on with their job in spite of knowing they had lost old friends and members of their own family.

THE GREAT WORK HORSE

Common Quay with the Old Custom House, Ipswich, in 1830, by W.S. Cowell, printers, Ipswich. The sprit of a stackie is left of the picture *

The sailing barge originates from the wooden lighter of the late 17th century, used to unload or 'lighten' coastal vessels which had to anchor in deep water.

A barge is essentially a flat-bottomed boat built on a keelson. Thames Barges, referred to thus due to their concentration in that river are called sailing barges or spritsail barges, for their type of rig. They trace their ancestry back through 17th century Dutch Barges. Each has a distinctive shaped stem and transom, and has lea-boards which can be raised and lowered to prevent drift sideways. They are ideal for working in shallow waters, up the rivers and creeks of Kent and East Anglia where they can be beached, taking cargo from farms, rural wharves, creeks, backwaters, local ports and harbours, sailing through the channels of the Thames Estuary and up the London River to the docks. Carrying grain, hay for London's horses, timber, bricks, stone, sand and gravel one way, the barges returned with materials for brickwork, cement, animal feeds, fertiliser, paraffin, coal and acid for heating and processing, a constant cycle of general trade.

The Thames sailing barge was the predominant great work horse of coastal transport until well into the 20th Century. The distinctive rig and red sails were a common sight along the East coast of England, along the Suffolk and Essex coast, across to North Kent and up the Thames to London and, rarely, in France.

Here we shall refer to those that did not have an engine, but used wind energy alone as a sailing barge (s.b.), and an auxiliary barge (a.b.) which carried engine and sails. Most motor barges, (m.b.) had been de-rigged and used only motor power, save a few purpose built and one that has no power at all is a dumb barge (d.b.). The mulie rig applies to barges whose mizzen is not rigged with the normal sprit and gaff, but with a gaff and boom rig. A barge-master is called variously, skipper, master or captain. Here we refer to 'skipper' as did Frank Carr, a leading authority in the barge world.

Old Bourne Bridge Ipswich, in 1851, by Henry Robertson showing the hard on the far side of the river at the bottom of the dirt road. Corn crops were brought down that road to load onto old type barges. The copy was given to me when it was owned by John Corello. It is now owned by Ipswich Museum.*

Stackie barges had a very wide beam so they could carry a stack of straw or hay. Loads for horse feed bound for London were stowed in the hold and a stack of up to 50 tons was built on deck to mid-way up the mainmast. A platform could be created by extending planks over the rails. They had a very shallow draft so they could access creeks right up to the farms of East Anglia. The stackie barges had special mainsails and foresails that could be adjusted so that only half the sail was set above the stack. When loaded the man at the wheel or tiller could not see where he was going so although he was familiar with the routes his mate had to stand on the stack and shout down to him so that he could steer. It was a unique and skilled trade.

Barge unloading manure at Waldringfield on the River Deben. [+]

In the 19th century commercial brickyards were hard at work to supply the materials to build whole streets of terraced houses in fast expanding industrial London. Barges carried loads sufficient to build one house, returning with manure from London horses to be used for making more. For example, Waldringfield anchorage on the Deben saw Thames barges at the quay and pier for the Cement Works.

They moved the grain from square-rigged grain ships from Australia or Canada to flour or animal feed mills in East Anglia. [+]

The new Ipswich Lock c 1842 [*]

Off Northfleet 1890's

The depression of the mid 1930's proved the death knell of the trading barge. Numerous barges were moored on the "starvation" buoys off Woolwich for weeks on end waiting for a cargo. Others were left on river banks, their crew walking home, when there was no cargo to be had. At the same time the motor lorry was growing in popularity, as was other mechanised farm equipment. Many of the smaller barges were abandoned pre-war, apart from a few which were used as lighters. Often the family lived on a barge, there was no option, they couldn't afford anything else, and the family crewed. That could mean that youngsters grew up with no schooling, so many of them were illiterate. During the lean 30's often there was no cargo for them, so no pay. A bargeman's family might be put into the workhouse when there was nothing to eat in the house, but you will have a job to find a family that will admit it now. *"Poor but proud, we were"*.

Sailing barges had last taken part in sea warfare during the Anglo Dutch wars between 1650 and 1680. Despite the advance in technology by 1939 the Navy actually asked for their services again. Incredible!

During the whole of the Second World War the humble Thames Barge continued to play a vital role. Goods imported into England cost a huge number of ships and lives lost. There was a government campaign for not only farmers but every family with a garden or allotment to 'Grow for Victory'. Troop movements dominated railway trains, our road network was poor and petrol was rationed. The Thames barge, which had been in decline, now became important to the merchant marine as other merchant ships were converted for a military use. Few barges had engines and still harnessed wind power. Older wooden barges were in particular demand for carrying ammunition and explosives as there was no risk of sparks etc to the dangerous cargo from an engine, and importantly they did not attract magnetic mines. A manpower bonus was that a Thames barge required only two people to sail, a skipper and often a boy or a woman, both useful as mates or third hands when fit adult males joined the armed services.

Barges were found to be particularly useful at Dunkirk as they could go right up to the beach to pick up the men. The sailing barges could then be abandoned because towing them home was going to use valuable tug time. They could be used as emergency embarkation platforms, makeshift jetties. Those with an auxiliary engine would take the troops directly off the beach to ferry them to the larger ships anchored off shore with hundreds of soldiers in their large hold or on deck. Big, slow moving barges made easy targets for the Luftwaffe. Later during the war barges were moored in the estuaries and on the south coast as anti aircraft/submarine/E boat lookout posts and to report German aircraft dropping mines into the sea. Others were moored in the Port of London with barrage balloons attached as anti aircraft devices or sailed all the way to Glasgow to supply the ocean liners that had been converted to troop ships.

Ipswich dockside, post war *

The war ended in 1945 but it was 1947 before the last sailing barge that had survived was returned to the owners. Most were then de-rigged and fitted with engines, and no more were ever built. Anyone trying to leave Felixstowe harbour under sail without engine power against the tide with an on-shore wind – or no wind at all - will realise the importance to those in trade to be able to deliver their goods more efficiently. In 1953 Ipswich had the largest fleet of barges in the country still in trade; you could walk across their decks from one side of the dock to the other. The few remaining today, re-rigged and used for leisure, are supreme examples of British working maritime heritage.

Despite this long history Bargemen were held in low esteem. Bill Polley, a skipper for Paul's:

"We would dress up of a Saturday, but none of the girls would have anything to do with us. We were just 'dirty old bargemen'. All the barge families knew each other, it was pretty much a closed shop; often they married each other, out of necessity really."

In May and June 1940 they earned their place in history.

PROGRESS AND RETREAT

In 1939 regular troops were based in the Far East or Mediterranean. We had sent the British Expeditionary Force (BEF), mainly new recruits, to fight in France hastily and too late having drawn from Britain the whole of the trained and equipped formations that were available.

On 11th October 1939 Minister for War, Hore-Belisha announced to the Commons that he had sent an army of 158,000 men to France, supported by lines of communication, a regular flow of supplies and munitions, 25,000 vehicles and specially equipped harbours. In fact many men had arrived with their unused weapons still packed in greased crates having never had the opportunity to fire them, or perhaps having fired weapons only once to complete the requirements of their basic training.

Major-General Bernard Montgomery, (affectionately known as 'Monty') 3rd division:
> "I was amazed to read ... the speech of the Secretary of State for War ...In fact ...the Army was totally unfit to fight a first class war on the continent of Europe ... Indeed the Regular Army was unfit to take part in a realistic exercise".

II Corps Commander, Lieutenant General Alan Brooke noted:
> "It would be sheer massacre to commit it to battle in its present state".

Angela:
> "My dad Cecil Mortlock told me that the destroyer 'Gallant' put to sea for active service with wooden guns on the foredeck to fool the Germans."

Bill:
> "There were 84 mock landing barges on the Orwell, 72 on the Deben to fool the Germans into thinking that D-Day was

going to be launched from Suffolk. They were made mainly of scaffolding and canvas, assembled at night, and local people popped down to hang their washing out so that enemy planes would see signs of life. At the end of the war the ministry sent a team down to dismantle them, which they did, leaving the plywood and timber on the beach. The following week lorries came to collect it and found the tide had washed it all away. By co-incidence nearly every back yard on the Shotley peninsular had a shed or a chicken hut on it!"

By May 1940, following the Nazi invasion of the Low Countries, support for Prime Minister Neville Chamberlain's leadership had fallen to almost nil. Inevitably King George VI accepted his resignation. Winston Churchill drove to Buckingham palace on the 10th May. King George VI asked him to form a government. The astute Churchill appointed a coalition government, for in times of great danger to the nation he knew that the good of the country must come before politics. Now Britain had a man with the imagination and flair that had been lacking.

Churchill, 10th May 1940:

"... as I went to bed at about 3a.m., I was conscious of a profound sense of relief. At last I had the authority to give directions over the whole scene. I felt as if I were walking with destiny, and that all my past life had been but a preparation for this hour and for this trial. Eleven years in the political wilderness had freed me from ordinary Party antagonisms. My warnings over the last six years had been so numerous, so detailed and were now so terribly vindicated that no one could gainsay me. I could not be reproached for making the war or with want of preparation for it. I thought I knew a good deal about it all and I was sure I would not fail....facts are better than dreams".

On the same day Hitler's armies struck westwards across Europe. Within three weeks Holland and Belgium had surrendered and

German Panzer (tank) divisions had split the British and French armies.

'Winnie' 10th May 1940 [1]

Churchill spoke to the House of Commons as Prime Minister for the first time on the 13th of May, to announce the formation of the new administration:

"I would say to the House, as I said to those who have joined this Government: I have nothing to offer but blood, toil, tears and sweat. We have before us an ordeal of the most grievous kind. We have before us many, many long months of struggle and of suffering. You ask, what is our policy? I will say: It is to wage war, by sea, land, and air, with all our might and with all the strength that God can give us; to wage war against a monstrous tyranny never surpassed in the dark, lamentable catalogue of human crime. That is our policy. You ask, what is our aim? I can answer in one word: It is victory, victory at all costs, victory in spite of all terror, victory, however long and hard the road may be."

The 16th May saw the BEF starting to withdraw from its position east of Brussels, in the face of German attacks.

By the 19th May the BEF Commander, General Gort, was cut off from his supply dumps.

Daily Express Friday 31st May 1940:
"When the terms of King Leopold's order to the Belgian troops to lay down their arms were learned in Paris today they aroused indignation. It was seen that the entire equipment of the Belgian army, most of which was made in France, should fall into German hands. The terms are said to be:-
Troops are forbidden to move from their positions at the time of capitulation:
Troops are to line up at the roadside, leaving routes clear:
They are to notify their positions with big white boards:
They are forbidden to destroy any arms, munitions or supplies.
It is noted that the capitulation was not countersigned by General Michiels, Commander-in-chief of the Belgian Army, nor by General Desrousseaux, second in command."

In the ranks of the BEF bellowed commands by sergeant majors did little to lift the spirits of men who recognised defeat.

Brian Horrocks in his autobiography, 'A Full Life' (1960):
> *"If you ask anybody what they remember most clearly about the retreat to Dunkirk they will all mention two things - shame and exhaustion. Shame as we went back through those white-faced, silent crowds of Belgians, the people who had cheered us and waved to us as we came through their country only four days before, people who had vivid memories of a previous German occupation and whom we were now handing over to yet another. I felt very ashamed. All I could do as I passed these groups of miserable people was to mutter 'Don't worry, we will come back.' Over and over again I said it. And I was one of the last British most of them were to see for four long years. We had driven up so jauntily and now, liked whipped dogs we were scurrying back with our tails between our legs. But the infuriating part was that we hadn't been whipped. It was no fault of ours."*

Europe woke to news of a resounding victory in Belgium by Hitler and his team. Steam engines blustered at railway stations as troop trains moved forward. There were statesmen like admonitions on the inadvisability of defying the 3rd Reich.

At the outbreak of the allies' war with Germany the Axis had more aircraft and more men in service. Allied leaders tended to be conservative, lacking in imagination. The Germans had flair and took risks. Attacks are planned ahead and can be bold. Defence is reactionary, always catching up with thinking done 'on the hoof'.

Civic buildings were fast deserted, bank records hastily crammed into suitcases, the conscientious clerk aboard the last few trains heading south.

*By 22nd May the allied armies were in full retreat, hindered by roads and railways clogged with civilian refugees.*²

German advance force. [2]

Another chap told us about the retreat from Belgium:

"We walked for miles. We had no food or water; we had to scrounge what we could. We knew people had hidden things in their houses so we prodded around in the smoking abandoned farmhouses and found some wine and water. There were abandoned trucks with stuff in them although the RASC were coming behind us blowing up or burning

everything. When I got to the 'Maid of Orleans' moored in the inner harbour I still had a large lump of fruit cake."

An RASC sergeant had been supplying ammo:
"I had it with me in my truck. We had been ordered to disable the truck, but we thought that was daft so we brought it through and supplied the guns on the beach".

23rd/24th May 1940: With the Germans now at the French coast it was possible, from Vice-Admiral Ramsey's office on the cliffs of Dover to hear the shell bursts of the attack of the 2nd Panzer Division on Boulogne. The channel ports fell into German hands one by one following a gallant and bloody defence.

Lt Gen Brooke was covering the retreat to Dunkirk with three divisions. Bugley-Thorne, commanding one of them, found himself facing a large number of German tanks.

Churchill gave orders to the garrison at Calais to fight to the last man, in order to give time for the troops to embark at Dunkirk. The tanks in the area went off to fight that battle, delaying the fall of Calais and giving time for the evacuation at Dunkirk. If Calais had surrendered the German tanks and troops would have been freed to attack the men making for the beaches and most of them would never have got away.

Winston Churchill:
"It was my decision. When I gave those instructions to the men at Calais I thought I was going to be sick. At one time I thought we should be lucky if we were able to get 40,000 men away. Next morning my price went up. The small boats taking away our army; it is an epic tale....It was the magic carpet by which this great host was collected from Dunkirk and distributed overnight, as it were, all over the country. It was my job to keep the Germans out."

British troops defending Calais – "at all costs" [2]

The Germans sent a messenger under a flag of truce offering surrender to the Allied forces around Calais. The German War diary records with admiration the unequivocal 'No'.

Daily Express 31st May 1940:
   "Little British Garrison in Calais never gave in."
   "The steadfastness of a small force which was sent last week to hold Calais is hailed in a War Office communiqué last

night, which says their action 'will count among the most heroic deeds in the annals of the British Army.'
They were ordered to attack and to maintain communication with the BEF. But, faced with strong German mechanised forces, they could do neither of their tasks.
They concentrated instead on the defence of the town. Attacked time after time, and bombed and shelled continuously, the little garrison held out for several days. The War Office says:-
'By it's refusal to surrender it contained a large number of the enemy, and was of invaluable assistance to the main body of the BEF in it's withdrawal to Dunkirk.'"

A decisive factor was that Generalfeldmarshall von Rundstedt, realising that his heavy armament had outstripped its supply lines, ordered a halt to his tanks on 23rd May, validated next day by Hitler. The decision was made easier by Head of the Luftwaffe, Hermann Goering's boast that his Luftwaffe was going to finish off the British without help from other forces. Also the heavy armament was needed to take Paris, the key to total defeat of France, and so on to the rest of Europe. The air force of course was dependent upon the weather. Hitler's order to continue to advance, given on 26th May had come too late, allowing the Allies a few days to construct defences to enable the BEF to retire to the sea. It proved a serious error of judgement because in those four days the BEF maintained an escape corridor running North-West from the region of Lille towards Dunkirk. It was one of the major mistakes the Germans made in WWII.

The BEF was put on half rations. It became evident that a full scale evacuation was going to have to take place. The Gare Maritime at Dunkirk was bombed but the quay still stood and hospital ships took off thousands of French and British wounded, plus civilian evacuees, whilst under a curtain of fire from air raids, anti-aircraft guns, ships guns and shore batteries. The Cross-channel steamer *ST. HELIER* alone, for example, took

1,500 British and French this day. The British Destroyer *WESSEX* was lost, and the Polish destroyer *BURZA*.

Winston Churchill:
> *"Dunkirk was a turning point. In a month after their return to England these men became a formidable army. It was one thing to plan an invasion of England before Dunkirk, with a hundred thousand men; quite another when perhaps half a million would be needed to break down the defences of this army."*

The withdrawal from Dunkirk beaches was a huge operation carried out under relentless attack by enemy aeroplanes. It was not carefully planned in advance, but if you like 'cobbled together in haste by men on the spot' in the thick of the uproar and bloodshed, and yet it was managed brilliantly. The port itself was partly blocked by the sinking of concrete filled block ships. The sea gates and lock mechanisms were destroyed. One mistake in the handling of a ship could have blocked any vital channel as the access to the sea shrank until finally closed and the British and French armies retreated to the beach.

The credit for the pulling together of the people and ships to achieve 'the miracle of Dunkirk' was due to Vice-Admiral Bertram Ramsay at Dover, who spent those nine days in sparse accommodation in the bowels of the chalk cliffs of Dover, below the castle, in the Dynamo room. After reaching the top of the rear-admirals' list in October 1938, the Royal Navy had elected to move him to the Retired List. With relations with Germany deteriorating in 1939, he was coaxed from retirement by Winston Churchill in August and promoted to Vice- Admiral commanding Royal Navy forces at Dover. A brilliant decision, for Ramsey was both an astute judge of men and an organiser: his leadership exercised his ability to find the right men and trust them to do their job, whilst overseeing every aspect of the operation.

Dover harbour is graphically described by the Master of the tug *SIMLA*, Mr. G. D. Lowe, in 'The Nine Days of Dunkirk':

"The fortnight commencing the 20th May 1940 at the time of the evacuation, the tug SIMLA assisted inside and outside of Dover Harbour, 140-odd ships being moved. The crew and myself were practically on our feet night and day. I have great praise for my crew. Never a grumble, but carrying on with the good work, all longing to help as much as possible, to see our soldiers home safe.

"On 22nd May when attending to harbour work, I received a signal, that a French ship, the s.s.THEMSEN, with refugees on board, had been in collision with a British ship, the s.s. EFFORD three miles south west of Dover. On arriving there the EFFORD had sunk, and the crew on her were in one of her lifeboats which I picked up. I found out from the captain that all his crew were saved and that the THEMSEN had cut right into his ship.

The tug SIMLA took the s.s. THEMSEN in tow, and I went on board of her, while my mate took charge of the tug, for the captain of her was in such a nervous condition that he could not take charge of his ship. He had just come from Dunkirk after being bombed all day and he asked me to take charge of his ship.

"The tugs had orders to shift two destroyers from Admiralty pier on 24th May in the early hours of the morning to make way for other ships to berth. They were the H.M.S *WHITSHED and VIMY, but the crews of the destroyers were so tired and exhausted from their recent experience at Dunkirk that we let them sleep on , and shifted the destroyers without them. I expect that when they turned out from their much needed sleep, they were surprised to find their ships in a different position, but they were all fresh to go to sea again and carry on the good work.*

"During the very dark night of 24th May, the s.s. KOHISTAN (5,884 tons) was outside, waiting to berth at Admiralty pier.

She had about 6,000 troops on board. The naval people wanted her to berth as soon as possible on account of enemy planes coming over. The job of berthing her was not an easy one, for the harbour was full of other ships, no-one being allowed to show any light. It was just like going into a thick fog. You could not see the other ships or buoys in the harbour, and it was a great worry trying not to hit other ships. First we would scrape along one destroyer then just miss another one by a few feet".

MILITARY DISASTER

On 25th May 1940 Boulogne was captured. The Allies were in disarray; British Prime Minister Winston Churchill received a stark message from French Premier Paul Reynard:
"We have been defeated".

The waterworks and mains at Dunkirk were destroyed. Although many of the BEF had been taken out of the port, remaining troops now had no water except a few brackish wells on the perimeter. The water boats *GOLDEVE* and *CLAUDE* were despatched.

s.b Claude on the River Thames. Notice the row / bum boat with the name E.BALLARD. The Ballards were watermen and lightermen between the 1700's and the early 1900's [3]

s.b CLAUDE:
The sailing barge *CLAUDE* was built in Sittingbourne, registered at Rochester in 1876 for Charles Burley Ltd, Brickmakers and Cement manufacturers. A member of the Sargent family informed the Society for Sailing Barge Research (SSBR) that the *CLAUDE* was a water bowser, owned by the Sargents as one of a series to supply water to vessels lying in the Thames. She was not registered on the Merchant Navy List (MNL) of 1938 it is unclear

whether this was the vessel that was mentioned as despatched on 25th May to work in Dunkirk harbour. However the *CLAUDE* listed on the French wreck site is described as a sailing barge.

m.b.GOLDEVE:
The *GOLDBELL, GOLDCROWN, GOLDRIFT* and *GOLDEVE* were built at Faversham in 1932 for London-based sailing barge owner E J & W Goldsmith Ltd. by Pollocks. They were 94 ft long with a single mast driven by twin Bolinder engines. She came back from Dunkirk but sadly her captain Walter Charles Burt died or was killed aged 57 in 1942 while still on war service.

GOLDEVE was a 255 tons twin screw diesel vessel, rebuilt in 1949 (possibly when returned to her owners after the war). They all survived the war and were sold to Coastal Tankers Ltd. when *GOLDEVE* was re-named *LEASPRAY*, in 1952. She was later moved to the Clyde, re-named the *WARLIGHT* and served the Western Isles of Scotland. She was broken up in 1976.

24TH May saw the tug *FOREMOST 87* towing two barges. Although not named they may have been the two water boats, *CLAUDE AND GOLDEVE*. The supplement to the London Gazette of the 16th August 1940 mentions that the tug master, Captain James Fryer was awarded a medal for his part in the evacuation. Other than a brief mention by Tug *CERVIA* we have discovered no more information about which barges were towed by *FOREMOST 87*.

Calais finally surrendered on 26th May: The first elements of the evacuation plan went down in ruin. Winston Churchill said in the House of Commons:
> "The events in France are a colossal military disaster - the whole root and core and brain of the British Army has been stranded at Dunkirk and seems about to perish or be captured".

Not wanting to undermine the morale of the nation, the government did not publicise the full extent of the unfolding disaster around Dunkirk. However, the grave plight of the troops led King George VI to call for an unprecedented week of prayer. Throughout the country, people prayed on 26th May for a miraculous delivery. The Archbishop of Canterbury led prayers *"for our soldiers in dire peril in France"*.

Prayers were offered in synagogues and churches throughout Britain that day, leaving the public with little doubt about the desperate plight of the troops, sons, husbands and brothers.

The Admiralty made the signal *"Operation Dynamo is to commence."* Our forces were in flight.

The last week of May thousands of British and French soldiers were on the beach at Dunkirk. About 400,000 BEF and associated French and Belgian troops had been confined to a pocket about 20 miles wide and 30 miles long in the region of Dunkirk, the perimeter of which shrank in planned stages towards the beach, up to 4th June.

They were up to their necks in salt water, eddying and flowing up and down with the tide like so much flotsam, seeming from afar like strings of seaweed.

Hour after hour they waited, day following day, in orderly lines as they had in the Jarrow marches, as they had queued at the dole office during the depression, at the pit head when the general strike ended, at the factory gate, at the soup kitchen, at the bus stop when they eventually found work, at the recruiting office, at the railway station, at embarkation and as they had when they marched into Belgium, and out again before a relentless enemy.
Imagine if you can how filthy the men were, sand inside their clothes, battledress caked with salt as they waded into the water and out again time after time. They must have stunk.

Men were drowning coated in thick oil, or exhausted by the weight of their sodden wet thick uniforms, too tired even to get rid of them.

Terry's dad didn't talk about it much:
> "The thing that I can't forget is the smell. We were in battledress. When it gets wet it weighs a ton. In and out, in and out, up to our necks, some of the men got so tired they just slipped under as the tide rose. There were others killed by enemy fire of course. We pushed aside the bodies as they floated by, but the smell of the dead and the blood – that's what I can't get out of my mind".

Local messages from Dunkirk itself to Dover were agitated and inaccurate, causing almost complete confusion. The convoy approaching Calais, which lay under a heavy pall of smoke, turned back. Two destroyers were engaging shore batteries. Ships were obliged to pick their way between the numerous wrecks which were making navigation hazardous.

A secret cipher telegram was sent by the War Office to the Admiralty on 26th May stating that the emergency evacuation of troops from the French coast was required immediately.

Initial plans called for the recovery of 30,000 men from the BEF within two days, at which time it was expected that German troops would be able to block further evacuation. Only 25,000 men were brought off the beaches during a 24 hour period, while 35,000 could be brought off the East Mole, a pier built on a breakwater protecting the outer harbour. Ten additional destroyers joined the rescue effort on 26th May and attempted rescue operations in the early morning, but were unable to closely approach the beaches, although several thousand were rescued.

Many were regulars, who had joined up to take the King's shilling rather than go down the mine that had taken the lives of their fathers with disease or disaster, who had shared a pair of stockings with their sisters because mum couldn't afford two pairs, who couldn't go to school because they had no shoes or who had spent months in the workhouse when their desperate parents could not feed them.

A vital factor in the initial part of this final evacuation, it is essential to picture in our minds an outer breakwater to the harbour known as the East Mole. It was not a stout stone breakwater with mooring places for ships. It was a spindly concrete pier with a wooden walkway barely wide enough for three men to walk abreast. There were emergency mooring piles, and at the end a 'nose' on which stood a short lighthouse. It was never designed to have ships docking against it but it was found that it could be used.

Dunkirk – British Naval ships and the East Mole [2]

The free movement of the tide beneath the piles made it difficult to bring craft alongside, and little or no room for manoeuvre in almost impossible conditions. It was not clear whether the Mole would stand up to the strain of ships berthing alongside but in the event it did, although there were limits to the number that could be berthed simultaneously. The large tidal fall – about 17 feet – also caused difficulties.

The only other option left was to evacuate the troops from the open beaches to the North-East of the town and both embarkation points were to be used almost continuously during the remaining eight days of the operation, except the last three when German air attacks intensified and Vice-Admiral Ramsey ordered night time sailings only.

As an embarkation site the beaches left much to be desired; the possibility of full scale evacuation from them had not been seriously considered. Larger vessels had to anchor half a mile out because of shallow water, sending their beach boats ashore to bring the waiting troops off. There would be extreme danger to the naval vessels in any case, as they would be sitting ducks. The tide ran swiftly, so that a soldier with waterlogged battle-dress had no hope of swimming. Dinghies and ship's boats were frequently capsized though overcrowding, especially during the first days before the beaches became organised.

Cecil Mortlock was serving on the destroyer *GALLANT*:
"I was Coxswain of the first longboat on to the beach. It was dusk. Dunkirk was on fire; fires were blazing everywhere. The noise of the guns, and bombs exploding was deafening. We went in under a pall of smoke without being able to see the beach. We didn't know whether the figures we could see ahead were Germans or British. But we knew our lads were out there somewhere so we just had to chance it. As we neared the beach in the middle of this hell we crept even slower, crouched down hoping to get away quick, and we

heard a Cockney swear! The men made a rush for us, we got as many on board as we could and told the others we'd be back and that's what we did, back and forth until the GALLANT was so low in the water she couldn't take any more, and made our way back to Dover".

A soldier:
"Like ectoplasm, out of the early morning mist came a shape, we didn't know what. We fell silent as it got nearer, holding our breath".

During the day improvised jetties were built out of abandoned lorries and stranded boats acted as staging points. Over a 24 hour period 25,000 men were able to be rescued from the beaches. In the same period perhaps 35,000 men would be picked up from the mole. The urgent need for shallow draught boats became obvious.

Rescue was on its way. The movement of the Little Ships had begun.

OPERATION DYNAMO

Vice Admiral Bertram Ramsay had been given less than a week to prepare the operation. It took its name from the room in the naval headquarters below Dover Castle, which contained the dynamo that provided the building with electricity during the war. It was in this room that Ramsay planned the evacuation and briefed Winston Churchill as it was under way.

From his headquarters in the tunnels beneath Dover Castle, he directed and inspired a small staff who had the awesome task of planning the evacuation of up to 400,000 British and French troops under constant attack from German forces. By 26th May Ramsay had assembled 15 passenger ferries at Dover and a further 20 at Southampton. These it was hoped would be able to embark troops direct from the quays at Dunkirk. To help in the evacuation and to provide escorts for the merchant ships Ramsay had a force of destroyers, corvettes, minesweepers and naval trawlers. These ships were augmented by cargo vessels, coasters and some 40 Dutch self-propelled barges.

Apart from normal navigational hazards such as sandbanks, wrecks, floating debris and fog the rescue force had to face relentless attack by the German Air Force, shelling by German coastal batteries at Calais, Gravelines and Nieuport, by now all fallen. There were torpedo attacks by U-boats and E-boats, and magnetic mines, including new ones dropped throughout the evacuation. Evacuation convoys from England were forced to take longer routes to Dunkirk. The Navy managed to sweep three channels to keep them relatively free, known as routes X, Y and Z. The first convoy, after sustaining heavy air attacks, found the port of Dunkirk and its oil tanks ablaze and only the passenger ferries *ROYAL DAFFODIL* and later the *CANTERBURY* succeeded in berthing. On that first day only 7,500 troops had been rescued and it was clearly impossible to use the port which was now reduced to rubble and littered with wrecked shipping.

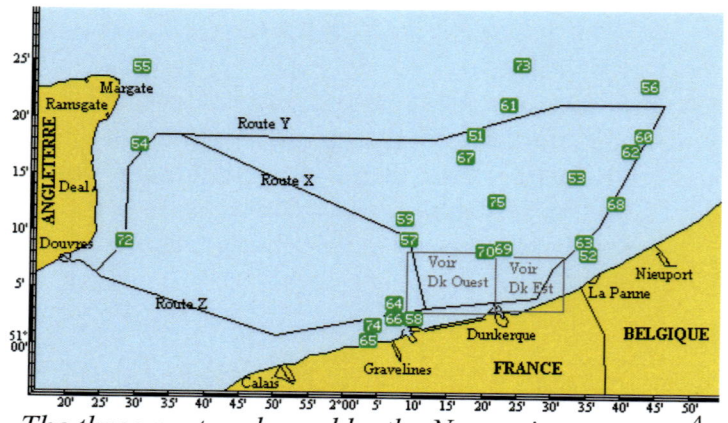

The three routes cleared by the Navy minesweepers [4]

Although the British Merchant Navy totalled some 10,000 ships, the necessities of war meant that all of them were transporting, loading or discharging urgent cargo, so that the number of available craft was small. How to get hundreds of thousands of men off open, shallow beaches, where they had no food or water, and had to defecate in the sand with no means of cleaning themselves, under relentless night and day attack from above? In addition, flat bottomed barges were required to run supplies of ammunition and drinking water on to the beaches, Dunkirk town's waterworks having been bombed on 25th May.

It was possible to hear the bombs in the silence of the cliff tops at Dover. And in the Dynamo room, realising that the moles would have to be abandoned, the staff began to plan for the use of the open beaches. The principal weakness of Ramsey's force at this moment lay in the lack of small craft. An urgent appeal was sent to the Admiralty for reinforcements.

The Navy's Small Vessels Poole had asked the BBC to broadcast a call on 16th May to *"all owners of self-propelled pleasure craft between 30 and 100 feet to send particulars to the Admiralty within 14 days"*. The Port of London had already established a tug pool and lighterage pool. Initially these vessels had been intended for work in British harbours, but the information collected now allowed large numbers of small craft to be assembled, mechanically checked and fuelled in time for the evacuation.

Some of the requisitioned boats returning up the Thames [2]

In some cases the owners could not be contacted and boats were taken without their knowledge - such was the speed and urgency of the operation. The River Emergency Service for the Upper Thames and through them Toughs Boatyard at Teddington did sterling service in requisitioning suitable motor yachts, with or without the owner's permission!

Douglas Tough of Tough Brothers together with Ron Lenthall collected many of the boats on the upper reaches of the Thames. They reported that the owner of one of the boats which was being commandeered could not be contacted but, hearing that his boat was being taken away, had informed the Police that it was being stolen and they pursued it to Teddington Lock.

More than 100 craft from the Upper Thames were assembled at Tough's Ferry Road Yard. Here everything unnecessary was taken off and stored. Bob Tough, son of Douglas and a past Commodore of the Association of Dunkirk Little Ships (ADLS) has lists of china, cutlery, pots and pans etc. all taken off and stored and returned to the owners in due course.

These small boats were joined by lifeboats, trawlers, tugs, lighters, Thames barges, pleasure steamers, motor yachts, launches, lifeboats, dinghies and other small craft. Some were commercial vessels from as far away as the Isle of Man and Glasgow. These smaller vessels were able to move in much closer to the beaches to lift troops who were queuing in the water, some of whom stood shoulder-deep for many hours to board the larger vessels. Thousands more were taken in these little ships back to Britain.

Gerry Barnes remembered:
> "I saw them go. I was a boy of eleven. We were only going to school half days because of the emergency. We heard they were going so some of us went down to Pier Hill, above Southend Pier, at 8 o'clock in the morning. There were cockle bawleys from Leigh-on-sea which we knew well, and all sorts of others coming down the Thames. We looked out for the ones we knew, like the ROYAL DAFFODIL, ROYAL SOVEREIN, CRESTED EAGLE and GOLDEN EAGLE, day trip boats. My parents had taken me from the pier across to the Medway on a day trip on the MEDWAY QUEEN and she

was there. She fell into disrepair after the war and is being restored now.

The cockle bawleys had a superstition that if the hatch cover was put back the wrong way round it was bad luck. The crews were almost all in charge of a naval officer and the officer on RENOWN did place the hatch cover wrongly. She hit a mine.

"There were crowds and crowds of boats coming down in long streams that summer day. We had been used to seeing the Royal Navy fleet at anchor lined up on the Thames; it looked like that in miniature."

There was a fund raiser after the war. The people of Southend raised enough to buy a replacement. They gave RENOWN II to the families, the Osbournes, the Dents and the Noakes.

"Soon after that day the children were evacuated because the Germans were coming. Our parents took us, clutching our gas masks, to Rayleigh station at 6 am. Trains left every 15 minutes. Our school went through London to Queen Elisabeth School, Mansfield in Nottinghamshire, a mining town. It was a frightening but enlightening experience for us all. We stood in a row when we arrived late in the evening, waiting to be picked.

"Some of us, including me, lived with mining families in their small cottages, some went to the smart houses. My friend's parents were bombed and both killed. The people he was billeted with adopted him, paying for university after the war."

Captain Duggan, master of the Isle of Man packet boat *MONA'S QUEEN* described his experience as they neared the port of Dunkirk on 28th May:

"Immediately hell was let loose on our ship. We were shelled from the shore by single guns and from salvoes from the shore batteries. Shells were flying all around us; the first

Modern Frith's postcard 52171 of Mona's Queen (2) departing Fleetwood

salvo went over us, the second astern of us. I thought the next would hit us but it dropped right under our stern. The ship was riddled with shrapnel. Then we were attacked from the air. A Junker bomber made a power dive towards us and dropped five bombs but he was off the mark too, about 150 feet from us, all this while we were still being shelled. The Junker that bombed us was shot down crashing into the water just ahead of us. Another Junker attacked us but he too was brought down in flames."

"Owing to the bombardment I could see that the nerves of some of my men were shattered. I didn't feel too well myself but I mustered the crew and told them Dunkirk was being bombed and was on fire. On being asked if they would volunteer to go in they did so to a man".

'Mona's Queen' struck a mine and sank off Dunkirk on 29th May with 24 of her crew lost. Survivors were picked up from her lifeboat by the destroyer 'HMS Vanquisher', 29th May 1940. Photo: Medway Queen Preservation Trust

That day 47,000 British troops were rescued in spite of the first heavy aerial attack by the Luftwaffe in the evening. Ships both large and small, were now targets for German fighters, bombers, submarines and coastal batteries.

John William Josh (Jack):

"I was skipper of a Thames barge operating around London and the east coast. I was ready to help evacuate our boys from Dunkirk and was taken onto one of the tugs. My brother Bill, aged 30, was skipper of a Tilbury Lighterage Company tug and my brother Joe, a 16 year old working on a Watkins tug called RACIA. We left London from the Thames in different tugboats. All of us ferried men from the shore to the larger ships. We didn't count how many trips we made to and from the shore or how many men we saved. All three tugs returned with no damage though, with no injuries to crew. We all worked on throughout the war and all survived".

Jack had at one time been skipper of the *LADY ROSEBERY,* and in 1940 was skipper of the *J.B.W,* named for her owner John Bazeley White, with 'Darkie' Tom Hills, a West Indian, as mate. She was a 72ft. sailing barge that sank on 15 July 1943 after striking a mine NNE of Maplin Buoy, Burnham-on-Crouch. T.J. Hills is named on the Tower Hill memorial. At the time Jack was in Scotland, in command of the tug *ABEL 2.* Young Joe, aboard

RACIA made three trips to Dunkirk, bringing home 423 British and French troops.

By 29th May there had been heavy losses in destroyers: *WAKEFUL*, *GRAFTON* and *GRENADE* were gone: *GALLANT*, *GREYHOUND*, *INTREPID*, *JAGUAR*, *MONTROSE* and *SALADIN* all damaged. At 8.00 pm it was decided to withdraw the eight modern destroyers left. The convoys, the Mediterranean and the defence of Britain would all require sea power. That meant that Ramsey now had only fifteen older large vessels effectively meaning one per hour, which could lift only 17,000 troops in 24 hours.

Admiral Ramsey believed in delegating responsibility to someone on the scene, rather than attempting to exert central control over a large operation. Accordingly at the start of the evacuations he had posted Captain W.G. Tennant to take command on the beaches. Tennant had gone ashore on the evening of 27th May as Senior Naval Officer to co-ordinate embarkation from the beaches.

Captain W.G. Tennant was appalled at the almost complete confusion. He first signalled for the rescue ships to be diverted to the beaches east of the town and quickly organised an orderly co-ordinated embarkation from the beaches.

The men queued for their lives. They queued to get back to Blighty, to fight another day, to defend their mums, their wives, their children and the homes they loved, because Britain was *theirs*. They were part of an empire, and to serve 'King and Country' was a responsibility that gave them a dignity that deprivation had sought to take away.

Early the next morning Tennant decided to experiment with the use of the East Mole. Differences in loading speeds were dramatic HMS *SABRE* took 2 hours to load 100 troops from the beach, but from the pier it took only 35 minutes to board 500 troops.

Queuing for their lives [2]

It soon became apparent that it was also necessary to have someone in control of the fleet of ships off Dunkirk, and on 29th May Frederick Wake-Walker, who had served in the Royal Navy since 1907, was appointed Rear-admiral, Dover, with command of seagoing ships and vessels off the Belgian coast, with Tennant remaining in command on the beaches.

Wake-Walker reached Dunkirk on the minesweeper *HEBE* early on 30th May and for the rest of the evacuation spent most of his time on HMS *KEITH* directing operations to small boats under constant fire. On 1st June the destroyer, his flagship, was sunk by enemy action, and from 2nd June Wake-Walker directed the ships from a motor boat in the harbour. He was appointed a Companion of the Bath for his role in the evacuation.

The first convoy of Little Ships sailed from Ramsgate at 10pm on 29th May and by the next day the Channel, in the words of Douglas Bader *"looked like the road to Brighton on a bank holiday"*. The Channel was full of mines. Most of the small craft headed for the beaches to act as tenders, while initially the larger trawlers and drifters loaded troops directly in Dunkirk Harbour, later anchoring off so that troops could be ferried to them. Many of them had never sailed out of sight of land before.

Few owners took their own vessels, apart from fishermen and one or two others. The barge skippers were employees of their company and the vessels part of the merchant fleet. Although some of the crews were volunteers, they were seamen qualified to sail various small vessels, most working in the home merchant fleet. The operation was remarkably well recorded and records exist of most of the Little Ships and other larger vessels that went to Dunkirk but inevitably there were some volunteers and indeed vessels that went without recognition in the haste and confusion of those nine days.

When the Netherlands were occupied by the Germans on 10th May some of their boats escaped to England. The Dutch shipping bureau in London sent thirty-nine Dutch coasters to assist. The flat bottomed Dutch coasters saved 22,698 men, losing seven boats.

The Royal National Lifeboat Institution (RNLI) sent nineteen lifeboats, those from Ramsgate and Margate taken directly to France with volunteer crews. Others sailed to Dover where they were requisitioned by the Royal Navy, which provided the crews. There was an emergency workshop to repair and fuel the little ships in Dover.

850 British vessels of every shape and size sailed to the rescue of our trapped forces. Small craft, some manned by civilians, together with naval ships plucked around 338,000 men (including 112,000 French and Belgian soldiers) from the beaches. It was the greatest rescue operation of a trapped army ever known. About 400 civilian craft took part in Operation Dynamo. Collectively they became known as "The Little Ships of Dunkirk".

Winston Churchill wrote about Operation Dynamo in his book The Second World War, published in 1949:

> *"Since May 20th the gathering of shipping and small craft had been proceeding under the control of Admiral Ramsay, who commanded at Dover. After the loss of Boulogne and Calais only the remains of the port of Dunkirk and the open beaches next to the Belgian Frontier were in our hands. On the evening of the 26th an Admiralty signal put Operation Dynamo into play, and the first troops were brought away. Early the next morning, May 27, emergency measures were taken to find additional small craft. The various boatyards, from Teddington to Brightlingsea, were searched by Admiralty officers, and yielded upwards of forty serviceable motor-boats or launches, which were assembled at Sheerness on the following day. At the same time lifeboats from liners in the London docks, tugs from the Thames, yachts, fishing-craft, lighters, barges and pleasure-boats - anything that could be of use along the beaches were assembled that night".*

Not all requisitioned craft went to Dunkirk. Some were found to be unserviceable on arrival at Sheerness. Others broke away from their tow and were damaged before leaving home waters. The crews of the small craft were often civilian volunteers, temporarily given a naval rank and commanded by Navy personnel. Once the nature of the emergency became known there was no shortage of men of all ages. Some boats were towed across the channel, some went in convoys, a few made their way independently. Mercifully the sea was calm throughout the evacuation; just as well because small boats broke adrift from their tow, others developed engine trouble.

By 29th not only Dover harbour was full: the Downs, the historic anchorage between the Goodwin Sands and the Kent coast was crowded with craft of all sizes, Ramsgate filled up fast, and from every port between Plymouth and Hull the stream had already begun.

The failure of German intelligence to inform their Admiralty of these movements is extraordinary. The failure to evaluate the messages that must have reached them from the panzer regiments at Calais, from the Luftwaffe, or from their E-boat patrols and to understand the nature of the enemy they faced, and his determination, was their second misjudgement. Perhaps they laughed at the notion of such small boats rescuing an entire army.

Only the extraordinary efforts of the Ministry and the incredible response of owners of British small craft and the miraculous, some said, weather conditions, made it possible for the right ships to be brought together at the right time.

a.b. *PUDGE*, s.b. *DORIS* & a.b. *LADY ROSEBERY*

On 29th May 1940, *PUDGE*, one of only a handful of barges fitted with an auxiliary engine, had transported linseed to Millwall, and was waiting at Tilbury for a load of wheat for Cranfields in Ipswich. Waiting for a cargo back to the Orwell she received unexpected instructions to proceed instead to Sheerness under tow.

PUDGE rebuilt 2001 [5]

Built in 1922 at Frindsbury on the River Medway in Kent by the London and Rochester Trading Company (LRTC) *PUDGE* was 68 tons, 84 feet and built of wood as a bowsprit barge (later modified). She was fitted with a three cylinder Bargus Co. engine in 1935.

At the outbreak of war the LRTC employed 160 craft – barges, motor barges, lighters and motor coasters: 108 were requisitioned, mostly for mine watching and powder work. 13 were converted to landing craft for the Normandy invasion. By the end of May 1940, at least 24 of the LRTC (later Crescent Shipping) barges had been requisitioned ready for war service. Not all were registered, being river barges. Two LRTC barges took part in the Dunkirk evacuation, *PUDGE* and *THYRA*.

PUDGE'S skipper Bill Watson, was an old timer and one of the senior skippers of the London and Rochester Trading Company (apparently he wore gold earrings; whether it was because the bargemen were water gypsies, carrying their wealth with them or, as someone told me, because they were a guard against drowning, I don't know). When the call came for her to be towed downriver, Capt Bill Watson and his mate, known as 'Old Dick' hastily got food en route at Tilbury. *PUDGE* was towed down river to Dover by the tug *OCEAN COCK*, along with the barges *DORIS, ENA* and *TOLLESBURY*, the latter skippered by Charlie Webb's brother Lem.

At 8.30am on 31st May at Dover all the sippers were summoned ashore; the naval officer in command asked for volunteers:

> *"Volunteers are wanted for Dunkirk. Nobody will be compelled, but we shall be very grateful if you will offer your services"*

There were 17 barges in Dover harbour that day, lying alongside the Prince of Wales Pier and every one of the skippers was ready to take his barge across.

They drew lots and six were selected for immediate service, the three auxiliary barges, *PUDGE,* THYRA and LADY *ROSEBERY,* and the three sailing barges *DORIS, H.A.C.* and *DUCHESS.* The three auxiliary barges proceeded out of harbour forthwith with the sailing barges in tow. *PUDGE, DORIS* and *LADY ROSEBERY,* in that order, were taken in tow by the tug *ST.FAGAN.*

The tug *ST. ABBS* was towing the other three.

The Saint class tug H.M.S. *ST. FAGAN* was built by Lytham Shipbuilding and Engineering Co. (Lytham, UK) as a fleet tug fitted for ocean service. She was launched in 1918, commissioned in March 1919 and used pre-war to tow practice targets for the capital ships to shoot at. She displaced around 860 tons, had a complement of 30 and mounted one 12 pounder anti-aircraft gun for defence. These tugs rescued damaged merchant ships and warships, towing them to a friendly port. They had a top speed of twelve knots.

ST. FAGAN [6]

The tug log tells us:
"An average speed of only 5 knots could be made as the tow had to be 'nursed' because of the wake caused by destroyers and other vessels passing at speed".

By 3 am on the morning of the 1st June, under cover of darkness, they were 3 miles east of Dunkirk. The noise of enemy aircraft and the explosions all around as bombs hit their target was terrifying. There the three barges were cast off from the tug.

Skipper Watson's report:

"*1ˢᵗ June 01.30. Arrived off Dunkirk beach during darkness. 03.50 The LADY ROSEBERY was ordered by the tug to tow the DORIS inshore. While proceeding to do so and while the PUDGE was starting up her engines the ST FAGAN was blown up by a bomb. The PUDGE picked up 1 stoker and the mate of the tug. The LADY ROSEBERY and the DORIS were also sunk in the explosion and the PUDGE picked up their crews."*

No mention is made of the third hand of *LADY ROSEBERY*, who was lost.

The Orde record states that *ST. FAGAN* was bombed by German aircraft. The ship collapsed and sank in a very short time. *PUDGE* was a little way away trying to start her own engine:

"*She went up in the air but by the Grace of God come down the right way up*" said Bill Watson.

When the dust had settled *ST. FAGAN* was sinking fast, *DORIS* was foundering. The survivors from the tug swam to *DORIS* and *LADY ROSEBERY*. *DORIS* was cut adrift and sank. *LADY ROSEBERY* soon went down. *PUDGE,* third on the tow line and furthest away had just cast off and was able to pick up survivors. The Orde record states that the barge crews were all picked up but we know this to be in error. It records that *PUDGE* then sailed.

Lt. Commander G.Warren M.B.E., R.N. together with P/O E.Bastable, Coxswain, had been aboard *ST. FAGAN*. He recorded:

"*1ˢᵗ June 01.30 – Dunkirk Harbour abeam.*

02.30 P/O Bastable took the skiff inshore to find a suitable position for beaching the barges.

03.40 One barge (LADY ROSEBERY) started for the beach towing the one (DORIS) without engines. Aircraft were heard overhead.

03.55 ST FAGAN hit by bomb (Other reports say she hit a mine). Big explosion occurred and the ship collapsed and sank in a very short time. I found myself in the water with my signalman and telegraphist, near the two barges, one of which was sinking slowly: these were reached with little difficulty and the sinking barge cut adrift."

Among the 17 of *ST. FAGAN*'s crew members killed were Stoker Frederick Hatch aged 22, Stoker Bernard McBride aged 40 from Hilsea, Leading Steward William Longley aged 44, and Stoker William Clark 22, from Milton. SPO Buckwell (number PK 59570) also perished in the attack. They are commemorated on the Royal Navy Memorial at Portsmouth:

"In honour of the Navy and to the abiding memory of those ranks and ratings of this port who laid down their lives in the defence of the Empire and have no known grave other than the sea..."

Of the 25 officers and men of the ship's company, 2 officers and six ratings were saved. *PUDGE* had immediately launched her tender and picked up a stoker who had been on watch in the tug's stokehold when the force of the explosion blew him out through a hole into the sea. He now suffered a broken leg. As he was hauled out of the water the tug's mate also clambered in. A further six men, including her captain, Ltn. Commander G.H. Warren MBE, RN, climbed aboard a small boat and were subsequently taken aboard the tug *TANGA*.

PUDGE was now alone. Leaking badly from the shock waves from the explosion she could do little good by staying. A destroyer relayed the order for her to make for home with her rescued survivors and this she did.

TANGA had come across towing 6 small boats and had hung off outside Dunkirk waiting for troops to be brought to her. The crew of *ST. FAGAN* joined the 100 already rescued who were on board and all were returned safely home.

Tug *TANGA* was owned by William Watkins Ltd, her master H.P Gouge. Her logbook records that on the 29th May she had towed the barges *SNOWDON* and *SALADIN* to Ramsgate where they remained.

Report extracted from the logbook of the tug *TANGA:*
  "31st May 1940. 10:00 Anchored off Ramsgate
  14:00 Embarked 4 Lewis guns and 2 Gunners also Lt Cdr Sherwood RNR
  Proceeded with 6 boats (one of them a MLB in tow)
  Skipper A. Gardner RNR took passage in TANGA
  19:30 Air attack when nearing Dunkirk, near misses
  20:40 Off Dunkirk Harbour, proceeded 6 miles further east, slipped boats and hung off. Skipper helped to ferry troops in the MLB which however broke down and was abandoned
  Skipper Gardner returned on the 1st June in the M/S LEDA"
  "1st June 1940: 03:50 some of the boats returned with about 160 troops. Abandoned all but one motor boat and had to 'run for it'
  When abreast of Dunkirk Harbour picked up 6 men from a small boat - survivors of the tug ST. FAGAN
  A mile further on picked up the a.b. *PUDGE with 4 men on board. Took her in tow*
  09:00 Anchored off Ramsgate, motor boats came off and landed 160 troops
  16:00 Proceeded to Dunkirk towing 4 boats
  22:30 Arrived off Dunkirk, slipped tow and 'paddled about' outside"
  "2nd June 1940: 03:30 Ordered to 'clear out and run for it'
  None of the 4 boats had returned
  Other boats had brought the TANGA about 90 British and 80

*French troops
Proceeded towing a disabled M/B
08:00 Arrived Ramsgate, disembarked 170 troops"
"3rd June 1940: 16:30 Left Ramsgate towing the MADAME
SANS GENE and 3 M/B's
23:00 Arrived off Dunkirk, slipped tow and waited as before"
"4th June 1940: 02:00 The tugs SUN IV, SUN XV, RACIA
and TANGA were ordered to go alongside the pier and get as
many troops as possible. Embarked 37 troops
Ordered to 'clear out' none of the 4 boats towed over had
returned
02:35 Cleared the Pier Head., Air Attack – claim to have shot
down enemy plane
off North Goodwin Light Vessel took in tow a French fishing
lugger with a crew of three
04:00 Arrived Ramsgate and disembarked 37 troops
Total troops landed from Dunkirk 367"*

Photo Mick Wenban Jnr, believed taken from CHALLENGE, showing TANGA crossing to Dunkirk towing a string of lifeboats. In the background is the hospital carrier PARIS

The rally of the Little Ships in 1990 commemorated the 50th anniversary of the evacuation. Whilst *PUDGE* was moored in

Dover, Eddie Fry came aboard, wearing his medals. He was the 'boy', aged 14, on the Tug *TANGA*:

> "In England we had been told to round up anything that floated and tow them to Dunkirk Harbour. In the event we couldn't get into the harbour so we worked off the beach. We made three journeys across the channel, retrieving approximately 400 troops. It was on the second occasion we were crossing back to England we encountered PUDGE, at first thinking her deserted. They went in closer and I went aboard to take a line from TANGA. I found four stained, dripping wet khaki-clad exhausted men on deck. On looking into the hold I saw I reckon about 300 French soldiers, together with the rescued survivors from the explosion. TANGA took her in tow to cheers from below and three hours later we arrived safely in Ramsgate."

Other records do not mention the French soldiers and there is no record of *PUDGE* disembarking such a cargo.

Eddie was just a boy at the time and his memory may have played tricks, so that he confused *PUDGE* with another barge, although there is no mention in *TANGA'S* log of any other that he might have seen. *TANGA* rescued around 1,300 troops in all.

> "We were dive bombed by Stukkas ... you thought they were coming straight at you. It was horror. TANGA towed her through it all. I can't tell you how it feels for me to be standing here on her decks, her in such fine condition."

Eddie went on to become master of the *TANGA*. She was taken to the breakers yard in 1969 after a long period in Iceland and broken up in 1974.

An entry in the Ipswich Port Book shows that by the 23rd June 1940 *PUDGE* was already back at work. Capt. Watson unloaded a cargo of cottonseed for National Oil to leave Ipswich on 7th July

1940 at first light for Rochester. She loaded cattle food for BOCM, returning on 14th July. Research by Richard Smith through Ipswich Port Records, show *PUDGE* working in and out of Ipswich for LRTC (later Crescent Shipping) for much of her war service, mainly sailing between London and Ipswich.

From the 9th December 1940 she had regular return freights of flour from Cranfield Bros with return cargoes of wheat and one cargo of fertiliser from London for Fison Packard & Prentice at Cliff Quay on 15th April 1941. The following day she entered the dock on 16th April, and loaded flour from Cranfields. On 12th May 1941 she was noted as a motor vessel although she carried some reduced sailing gear until the end of the decade when she was de-rigged.

After the war *PUDGE* continued her work with the LRTC until 1968 when they decided to dispose of her. A rapid decision was made by the Thames Barge Sailing Club (Now the Thames Sailing Barge Trust) to buy her unrigged and straight out of trade after unloading her cargo of pineapple juice. Club members re-rigged her faithfully in accordance with her original design (minus bowsprit) with advice from professional barge skippers. PUDGE is now maintained by volunteers during the winter months and, thanks to enthusiastic fundraising by club members has received extensive restoration at Cardy's yard in Maldon, Rick Cardy's yard at Maylandsea, and by Tim Goldsack in Faversham. From May to October *PUDGE* is operated as a charter barge by the Trust from Maldon and Ipswich, sailing the rivers and coast of Suffolk, Essex and Kent. It is Trust policy to encourage passengers to participate in sailing as much, or as little, as they would like. It is probably the only association training keen members as future barge crews.

PUDGE is a member of the Association of Dunkirk Little Ships (ADLS). She is also entered on the National Register of Historic Vessels of the United Kingdom.

s.b. *DORIS:*
Built at Dock End Shipyard in Ipswich for Paul's in 1904, dimensions 84ft 62 tons *DORIS* was towed by the tug *ST. FAGAN* along with *PUDGE* and *LADY ROSEBERY.*

The approach to Dunkirk Roads was not easy in war time, with little if any light, the position of buoys uncertain, many shoals, dangerous minefields and strong tides. The tug captain, with no local knowledge and no charts had found difficulty in locating the inshore channel. However he brought the three barges to a position three miles east of the entrance to the harbour by daybreak. In the half light the crews could see little black spots on the sand which, in the improving light proved to be not ants but thousands of soldiers running down to the shoreline. High water would be about 8.30 so on a rising tide the barges could work their way well up the beach, discharge their cargoes and offer a chance of rescue to hundreds of men.

She was fatally damaged when *ST. FAGAN* struck a mine and was lost with all hands on 1st June 1940. Compensation of £970 was paid to Paul's. There are conflicting records concerning the barge crews. Skipper of *DORIS,* Fred Finbow (another source names Dick Finbow), is recorded as saved by Roger Finch, the mate Jack Grub was rescued by the crew of *PUDGE.* Tom Polley, a skipper for Paul's, had a young brother Dennis who was the cook aboard *DORIS* but was taken off at Dover before the crossing when he confessed to being under sixteen. Dennis continued on barges for most of his working life.

a.b. *LADY ROSEBERY:*
Registered number 127268, she was **a** vessel of 79 tons, built in 1917 at Rochester by Edward Packer of James Little & Co. for James Little. In 1928 she was owned by David J Bradley and upon his death in 1932, by Mrs Lilian Bradley of Rochester. She was fitted with a 3 cylinder 66 hp Kelvin engine. She is named in the 1938 merchant navy lists as registered at Rochester and

belonging to Samuel West, the barge builders and owners of Terrace Pier Wharf, Gravesend whose business started as Tuff, Miskin & West there in c.1902, becoming plain Samuel West in c.1906. They updated to a 4 cylinder engine, again a Kelvin.

LADY ROSEBERY [7]

Arriving off Dunkirk towed by the tug *ST. FAGAN* on 1st June 1940 she went down with her crew immediately following an explosion as the tug hit a mine. The cargo was lost. All the crew is recorded as saved by Richard Smith. We know the latter to be inaccurate as the cook/boy drowned. She is said to have turned over completely. Samuel West was compensated for her loss and the business survived until the 1950's.

WAITING.....

In the small hours, in the darkness there was a kind of peace. Men talked together, a voice called for a fag, there were cries of pain from the wounded, some voices cussing, but you could hear the rhythmic swish, swish, of the wavelets washing onto the seashore.

> *"The sea was like a millpond for most of those nine days. I remember looking over the side of the destroyer and seeing my face reflected in the water with the smoke from the stack behind me. It was like a mirror. There were not even any little diamonds in the water".*

Some men lay dreaming of home – fields of barley and wheat where poppies and cornflowers grew stood between hawthorn hedges layered in the old way. Shire horses pulled the plough in the early winter and women and children joined in the harvest. In dreams they could smell the straw and poppies and dust.

This night they waited.

Stomachs were cramped with hunger trying not to think of mums Yorkshires with thick brown gravy, or frying sausages. What were they doing now at home? It was Saturday, were they having a night at the pictures?

Ken Rudge:
> "I'd only joined up to get 'the King's Shilling' because there was no work in Slough. My father was a sergeant wheelwright in the Indian Army; he married my mother there and came home in 1914. Then he left. That meant my mother bringing up us four during the depression. It was not a cushy billet. She used to buy a pair of stockings, cutting them in half to make two pairs for my sister and me because she wanted us to be able to go to school. We went hungry too often. When I was a lad there was no work and the army offered three meals a day. My Dad had been in the King's Own Royal Irish so I went to join up but I was under age. The recruiting officer said 'Go down the road and come back when you are older.' So I did, I went down the road and came back saying I was old enough and I didn't have a birth certificate and he said 'Alright lad, sign there'. In spite of everything we suffered, the hunger, the thirst, being shot at, all of it, I don't regret a minute. It was just who we were. We weren't heroes either, some of us got up to some tricks."

A visitor to *PUDGE* in May 1990:
> "I am here today for Private Stanley Arthur Smith 7587791 Royal Army Ordnance Corps, attached HQ, 9th Infantry Brigade, who was 29 when he died on 29th May 1940. He was married to Vera, later living in Grundisburgh, in Suffolk. His parents were Arthur and May Smith.
> "He is buried at Oostvieteren Churchyard. I pray that he died recalling the shires and country lanes of England".

Excerpts from the notebook log of Desmond Hill, employed by the General Steam Navigation Company as a Second Mate a completely matter-of-fact account of the desperate situation. Desmond travelled to Dunkirk in one of the ships lifeboats towed by *SUN IV*. The log has kindly been made available by Camilla Disley, his granddaughter.

> "*Thursday May 29th 1940: Captain Watts phoned and asked if I was free and to go there (to Tilbury) at once.*
> *Phoned Mother: met me Hammersmith with gear. Pater also and take fond farewell of Margaret, quite convinced shan't see her again.*
> *5.40 pm In train: mixed feelings as to whether I'm a dammed fool or not; eventually decide its necessary to go and won't back out, feel rather heroic.*
> *Later: Quite a crowd gathered now and we get a Nelson speech from a very charming Rear Admiral. 8.45 pm Stopped for beer.*
> *At Tilbury go on to stage and find lots of volunteers, also lighter-men and bargees. More requests for engineers. Some go off in lifeboats, of which apparently unending supply.*
> *Go over and sign on at BOT. MM Office. Won't take me as charge-hand so signed as deckhand.*
> *Back on landing stage got friendly now with several decent chaps who I think want someone who knows the way to Dunkirk. All issued with tin hats.*
> *Friday May 30th 1940. 12.15 am: I am to be charge hand of boat; no cover but a dry boat. Now with Robert, John and Guss. Take on 40 gal. fresh water and large case of bully beef. Eventually push off and proceed down river 12 boats on "Sun IV". Divide up into 1hr watches afraid John did most of work that night.*
> *4.00 am Southend: stemmed tide and took on food:- 5 large loaves, 1½ lbs butter and marg, 20 tins of, sardines, soups, veal and ham roll, jam etc, Tea, sugar, milk etc. All hands long since frozen to the marrow but quite cheerful. Nice to be afloat again and glad I came.*

7.00 am Rounded NE Shingles - little convoys all over channel. Ropes are all doubled but keep breaking. Guss is well away in after locker. Still frozen. Other tugs stop now and then to pick up boats adrift.
10.30 am N. Foreland: dull and very cold: all curse weather. Have been eating breakfast on and off since 4 am: have some more. Cold salt water tea arrives in a dirty bucket.
11.30 am Anchored off Ramsgate - bearded Lt goes ashore and returns with charts and orders. We're to stay in the boats! Suddenly sun comes out and it's beautifully warm. All hands delighted. Have lunch again and some more tea comes round.
2.00 pm Left Ramsgate. Sighted fierce aerial battle. Plane in sea bombs dropped destroyer pompom.
7.48 pm 3½ miles off: temporary quiet. 2 planes in sea astern and on fire. Bomb just astern of Dest.
8.16 pm Our tugs machine gunned.
8.18 pm 2 Men overboard - one lost ... 8.58 pm Rounded No 5W Dunkirk Roads. Tremendous fires raging ashore, explosions all the time and a pall of smoke over everything hundreds of feet high. 2 paddlers just come out full of troops who gave us a cheer as they passed; all kinds drifters and odd craft about even the Portsmouth Isle of Wight car Ferry! Arial bombing getting less as light falls. Piers Head Lt still intact.
9.30 pm Tug anchored about 1m off shore. ¾ E of Pier Hds. Start sorting out boats. come alongside tug and lash up to a motor lifeboat with no rudder, we're to try steering both!
10.15 pm RNVR Lt comes aboard and we cast off. I find she steers quite well and makes about 3 knots. Strong ebb tide running. Very dark except for flashes from explosions.
Sound with an oar and anchor motorboat in about 8ft. Cast off and pull in. Hold her off just bumping: very slight swell and only small waves coming in, but quite enough - could do without any on this flat beach. Lieutenant goes ashore and in a few minutes we see a black mass show up dimly: so silent think they're Jerries and get all ready to pull like blazes. Hear Lt's voice and out comes first Tommy, they arrive in single file

and very orderly, an amazing effort in the circumstances since shells are landing all the time (from 15 miles away we afterwards learnt). One came just ahead when we left tug and another right between us and tug when ½ way to beach."

We were very busy most of the night doing 6 trips in all between tug and beach taking about 40 troops each trip. I never saw any of the other lifeboats - mine was the only one towed all the way back to England. Fantastic scenes at Ramsgate - all we wanted was to get home and go to sleep."

Dunkirk burning [2]

A British artillery officer produced an anonymous account of what it was like waiting on the beaches at Dunkirk on 30th May 1940. (Imperial War Museum):

"The whole front was one long continuous line of blazing buildings, a high wall of fire, roaring and darting in tongues of flame, with the smoke pouring upwards and disappearing in the blackness of the sky above the roof-tops.

Along the promenade, in parties of fifty, the remnants of practically all the last regiments were wearily trudging along. There was no singing, and very little talk. Everyone was far too exhausted to waste breath. It was none too easy to keep contact with one's friends in the darkness, and amid so many little masses of moving men, all looking very much alike. If you stopped for a few seconds to look behind, the chances were you attached yourself to some entirely different unit.

"A group of dead and dying soldiers on the path in front of us quickened our desire to quit the promenade.

"Stepping over the bodies we marched down the slope on the dark beach.

"Dunkirk front was now a lurid study in red and black, flames, smoke, and the night itself all mingling together to compose a frightful panorama of death and destruction".

British troops in retreat [2]

Another Englishman found a small boat on the beach:

"Several of us together managed to push it off. The engine wouldn't start so we paddled like hell with our tin hats, and were picked up by a Norwegian".

Left: Dover Harbour May 30th 1940 – note the barges lined up in the background, awaiting the call to duty.

a.b. *VIKING*

"*30th May. Went to La Panne and ferried all the forenoon. 31st The VIKING ran aground on the beach and damaged her bows and forward gears so that she could only go astern. She had 150 troops on board.*"

So wrote D. Gregory, the Master of a.b. *VIKING*.

Built at the Co-operative Barge Yard, Rochester in 1895 of pitch pine on oak, *VIKING* is 87 feet and 63 tons. She was registered at Rochester no. 104319; her first owner was William Jarrett of Upnor. In 1934 she had passed to his son, by which time she had been converted into a yacht barge, or ketch. Before WW2 she traded around the Medway and the East Coast, passing into the ownership of the Whiting family - well known Medway barge owners whose fleet numbered half a dozen vessels in the 1940s, although The MNL gives her owner in 1938 as P Tranter of Southend and describes her as a ketch, 50 tons, and he is named also in her Dunkirk log. After Dunkirk she continued her war service as a balloon barge, from which anti-aircraft barrage balloons were flown.

She had on board Sub-Lt T. R. Rumbold, Royal Naval Volunteer Reserve (RNVR) and is described as a diesel engined coasting barge.

Gregory continued:
"05:00 on 31st, between Dunkirk and La Panne the VIKING hailed the DWARF for assistance. 34 troops were transferred to the DWARF which took VIKING in tow. The tow rope broke but another attempt was made: in the course of the latter the tow rope fouled DWARF's rudder and could not be cleared. Proceeded about 2 ½ knots. About half way on the return journey, between Dunkirk and the North Goodwin the OLVINA took us in tow and DWARF proceeded independently. Wind now about force 3-4".

DWARF log records that the speed could only be 2½ knots.
OLVINA records:
31st May 11.20: The north-westerly breeze freshed to a force 3-4. Between Dunkirk and the N Goodwin L.V. took in tow from the DWARF the diesel engined Thames barge VIKING with 70 troops on board.

She sailed for Bray on 1st where she beached. She kedged off the following day and was towed to the Downs and then on to Ramsgate.

Southend Standard of 13th June:
"The engineer, Mr. Radcliffe estimates that VIKING saved about 1,000 troops by ferrying them off the beach to the waiting ships, as well as the 70 she brought all the way home."

DWARF: Tender to Sub-Marine Depot, Portsmouth. S/Lt D.A.O'Hare, MBE, RN.

"*31st May: Arrived Dunkirk – Ordered to La Panne. On the way the motor barge VIKING hailed for assistance. She had burnt out her clutches'* etc.

OLVINA – Trawler – Portland. S/Lt J.H.Cooper, RNVR, Unit Officer 40th A/S Group:
"*31st May: The north-westerly breeze freshened to a force 3 to 4, so OLVINA proceeded. Between Dunkirk and the N Goodwin L.V took in tow from the DWARF the diesel-engined Thames barge VIKING with 70 troops on board. Arrived Dover 22:00. Disembarked 244 troops. It was then ascertained from Captain A/P that OLVINA should not have gone to Dunkirk but should have been on A/S patrol.*

VIKING was then used as a balloon barge, flying anti-aircraft barrage balloons. After the war she was re-rigged at Whitstable to carry cargo as a coastal barge. At the end of that decade, Whitings was taken over by the London and Rochester Trading Company. Throughout the '50s VIKING worked for them.

Society for Spritsail Barge Research:
"*VIKING worked around the East and South-east coast ports: Norwich, Great Yarmouth, Ramsgate and Felixstowe, and twice crossed to Calais. With the London and Rochester she had Yarmouth - Dover limits, but a considerable diversity of cargo. This included imported grain and animal feedstuffs from London's Victoria and Millwall docks consigned to the merchants of Ipswich; Canadian and American wood pulp for the big paper mills, and sawn timber from Scandinavia and Canada for the traders at Maldon, Essex. On her return journeys she often carried bags of cement, destined for the emerging third world countries, for industrial buildings and new airports. In the late 1960's, VIKING was beached in the Medway."*

No longer sailing, she is laid up at Sittingbourne, Kent.

The French destroyer BOURRASQUE sinking after hitting a mine on 30 May 1940

THE AMAZING ARMADA

By nightfall on 30th May Dunkirk town was surrounded. The last men from Gort's headquarters in the town had to get away. They assembled at 9.30 pm, slipping away under cover of night. The last of them reached the perimeter at La Panne on 31st May. Gort himself left on Friday 31st May handing over command to General Alexander. He had requested that he stay until the operation was complete but Churchill emphatically refused. We could not afford to lose him, and it would have been a devastating coup for the Germans to capture him.

Sergeant Vickery from Ipswich was in the Royal Corp of Signals, working for General Gort in Dunkirk:

"I was told by my commanding officer to destroy everything. Me and my friend were among the last to leave. We had the use of a vehicle to get to the beach; near the beach we de-mobilised it and began to walk. We came across a post van that had been de-mobilised, the driver remaining with it. He had post to deliver to the boys, he said and didn't quite know what he should do with it. We had a look through and came across a parcel addressed to myself! It included a bar of chocolate my mum had sent me for my birthday. From that moment, until I was taken off the beach some days later, me and my mate rationed ourselves to one square each per day and that was all we had to eat, except on my 21st birthday on May 29th on the beach, I treated myself and my mate to two squares!"

His group went towards a longboat from one of the naval ships and the skipper said:

"Hang onto the back, mate, while the others climb aboard. Don't worry, I won't leave you behind'. So me and another chap did, but there were hundreds of men to get off the beach and the boat filled up. So the skipper said 'Hang on the sides, we'll tow you out'. He then told the other two on the boat to

hang on to me. 'And if you let go' he said 'You'll go into the water after him'.

"Of course we were all soaking wet, wading out into the sea in our battle dress, and I was sodden by the time they reached the battleship. We had to climb a rope ladder, and I got nearly to the top but I was so exhausted I just couldn't make it. I just clung to the ladder. A couple of sailors leaned over and hauled me up, saying 'Come on mate, you can make it' and when they got me aboard someone pushed a cup of hot chocolate into my hand. That was the best drink I ever had in the whole of my life".

His son has his father's Dunkirk medal:
"They didn't award one for a long time, because of course it was not a campaign, it was a retreat."

There was now nothing for it but to kick the dead off the mole, into the water.

"There were so many bodies in the water off the beaches that they were fouling the propellers of the smaller boats that got close to shore and we were under constant attack from machine-gun fire, bombing, explosions sending shrapnel in every direction".

Among the hundreds of vessels going to and fro across the Channel on the 31st May was the Thames Tug *TANGA*, towing 6 boats.
Tug *FAIRPLAY I* also arrived towing the sailing barge *BARBARA JEAN*, with tug *EMPIRE HENCHMAN* towing sailing barge *AIDIE*.

Tug SUN XII towed sailing barges *TOLLESBURY* and *ETHEL EVERARD*.

Tug *ST. FAGAN* towed auxiliary barges PUDGE, *LADY ROSEBERY* and sailing barge *DORIS*.

Tug *ST. ABBS* towed the auxiliary barge *THYRA* and sailing barges *H.A.C* and *DUCHESS*.

Tug *CERVIA* towed the sailing barge *ROYALTY*.

Tug *PERSIA* towed sailing barges *GLENWAY* and *LARK*.

Tug *FOREMOST 87* towing two sailing barges, not named. Most of the barges built for sail had not yet had auxiliary engines fitted. The tug *CHALLENGE* also towed an un-named barge and a.b *BEATRICE MAUD was* towed by one of the above.

Up to their necks [2]

a.b. *BEATRICE MAUD*

BEATRICE MAUDE heavy laden[3]

The yards of the White family, the son at Conyer and Faversham, his father at Sittingbourne in Kent, from the early 1890's until 1910, launched several fast craft. *BEATRICE MAUD* was built in 1910 by Whites as a speculation and registered in London (Official Number 129112). Length 88ft, 80 tons approximately.

She was the last to leave the Sittingbourne yard. She was bought by Kent Coasters Ltd., a consortium of traders from around Sittingbourne, for 4,000 guineas, her owner named in MNL as Samuel West in 1916. They traded until after the First World War when, during the depression trade dropped and she was laid up for lack of freights. Kent Coasters ceased trading and *BEATRICE MAUD* was bought by Alfred Sully in the name of Mrs. Jane Sully in the early 1930's, when her engine was fitted.

Her first master was Capt. 'Nobby' Finch from Mistley, known as 'Fat Nobby'. (Another 'Nobby' Finch skippered an Everard Barge) followed by Lionel Horlock. He was also from Mistley and a member of the Horlock family of bargemen.

J. Sully was her owner when, the log book of the Tug *SUN XII* records:

> '*Left Tilbury Docks at 23:00 on 29th May for Ramsgate towing the auxiliary barge THYRA and sailing barges ROYALTY, H.A.C. and BEATRICE MAUD: 12:10 on 30th May arrived at Ramsgate and was ordered to Dover: arrived Dover 15:00'.*

BEATRICE MAUD also was towed across the channel by an un-named tug, possibly *FOREMOST 87*, under the dull rumble of guns, on 31st May 1940 and was left stranded on the beach by her skipper, Lionel Horlock, as ordered.

Found on the beaches with no crew on board she had been brought back to England by some 300 soldiers, of whom 250 were French troops led by a Lieut. Heron who boarded her on 4th June, the final day of Operation Dynamo They had by now realised that all hope of rescue was gone. The opportunity offered by this big wooden boat was too good to miss. *BEATRICE MAUD* was located making for home under sail on 5th June in mid-channel with the 250 Frenchmen aboard. A British Naval ship towed her in to Dover the following day, 6th June.

She came home to Ipswich to be checked out, and on 20th August 1940 Harold Smy, living in Cemetery Road Ipswich was appointed her master, his mate being J. Cooper of Great Whip Street, Ipswich.

Before the war she had been a regular trader to Ipswich, Yarmouth, Battlesbridge and Snape, returning to a similar pattern after her adventures in France.

Harold Smy and BEATRICE MAUD after the war [8]

She then spent a couple of years loading brick rubble from the bombings in devastated London, bringing it away to Maldon, Mistley, Ipswich and Colchester during 1942/3. She sailed to Avonmouth with a ballast cargo of sand on 18th April 1943, berthing at Bristol on 1st June. Harold Smy, then her skipper, traded with Beatrice Maud to the northern coastal ports of the West Country and South Wales, including Minehead, Watchet, Llanellly, Port Talbot, Swansea, Cardiff, Newport, Barry, Penarth, Bridgewater, Gloucester, Bideford and Flatholm Island in the Severn. *BEATRICE MAUD* served as a stackie as well, shipping baled straw from Colchester to Ridham Dock in Kent for use in the paper mills. Many of the cargoes were foodstuffs, but there was also scrap-iron, steel and tobacco. She made her way back to London on 20th March 1946, where she loaded maize, arriving back in Ipswich on 28th March 1946.

She continued in trade for a while after the war, until faster, perhaps more efficient ships that could trade across the channel were called for. Barge masters retired; there were few new ones coming up, or the tradesmen working with wrought iron, brass or oak. Sailing barges were left in the muddy creeks of the East coast to rot away, the crews simply stepping off and walking home when they had no more cargo, or were sold off cheaply.

One barge fleet owner commented:
"No-one back in the '60's was as conservation-minded as we are nowadays, nor were we ourselves particularly interested in the old barges. It seems we were only too glad to get rid of them and didn't bother to retain any documentary record".

BEATRICE MAUD served as a barge yacht at Maldon and Faversham in 1986 and moved to Morwellham Quay between 1987 and 1993 to be used as a houseboat. In 1996 she was moved to Boating World Boat Yard, Landrake, Cornwall (On the River Lynher) where she was broken up by a wood reclamation firm in 2004. She is listed by ADLS.

The barge *PHOENICIAN* was moored to the quay outside the Ipswich Port Authority Custom's House for many years during the 1970's and 80's. She was owned by Albert Groom, who lived on her, with his tug *TID 172* tied alongside. He was an eccentric, colourful man, with a kindness and gentleness belied by his sometimes rough exterior. In 1981 or 1982 *TID 172* blew up with Albert on board.

Witnesses reported that one of her oil drums flew right over a nearby warehouse, landing in the road the other side! Albert emerged shaken but not stirred, black as the ace of spades, his clothing somewhat tattered, with a broken rib and surface burns. Albert died on 23rd January 1988 and *TID 172* was sold to a small group of enthusiasts by his executors. She is currently seen about the coastal rivers on occasions.

He wrote a small book of poetry, a copy of which he gave to the author during our many chats over a cup of cocoa as I stopped by on my way about my work.

One of Albert's poems follows.

> "There's an old Thames barge at Maldon Quay,
> Most of them have gone away but there's one perhaps you'll see,
> It's the BEATRICE MAUD, which like the dog, had her day
> In the war-torn days of Dunkirk, when all of us would pray
> For the thousands on the beaches, so many were slaughtered there,
> And the many who feared for their loved ones offered up a prayer.
>
> BEATRICE MAUD went across relying on sails alone
> Sitting duck for the enemy but proudly our flag was flown.
> She grounded and helpless was left there on the shore
> 'Midst the bombs and shells and bullets, the shrapnel and the gore.
> In the holocaust of wounded and dead how could any survive
> The horrors of Dunkirk? But many did, thousands came back alive.
> Later the tide rose, and somehow thro' the wrecks
> She floated, the men boarded her and safely below the decks
> They sailed her back. God was with her. Near three hundred were aboard.
> Near three hundred prayers were answered. It was the day of the BEATRICE MAUD."
>
> Albert Groom. C 1979

Not wonderful poetry, you might say, but written from the heart by man who loved barges and who lived through those fearful times.

*LATE ADDITION: For Lt. Heron's first hand account of BEATRICE MAUD's amazing escape, turn to page 244.

RECOLLECTIONS

Gravesend, 1935

Mr C.W. Wenban:
"I was a waterman who happened to be standing on the Royal Terrace Pier, Gravesend when I was asked if I was free to make up the crew of the Gravesend steam tug CHALLENGE: the job was probably connected with getting troops out. Of course I said yes. I went home to get a couple of shirts and a toothbrush and told Dorothy my wife what I was doing. Before long I was aboard CHALLENGE proceeding to Dover for orders. Once there under Captain C. Parker from Gravesend we were told to collect a barge loaded with supplies and tow it across for the boys trapped at Dunkirk.

"We got to Dunkirk and received directions to put the barge ashore further along the shore. So we steamed along to the position they said, but instead of British troops we found Germans had occupied the ground. We quickly turned about back to Dunkirk harbour and this time we were told to go to La Panne. CHALLENGE had just let go of the barge having run it at the beach at full speed ahead, when we watched a dive bomber come in to attack."

We are not given the name of the barge towed by *CHALLENGE* but it may have been *LUCY RICHMOND*.

Troops approaching CHALLENGE from the beach [6]

"The plane went for the barge and dropped a bomb which blew the barge right out of the water. There were five army men on the barge. According to my information only one man survived, and he was a Gravesend man who I later met in Dover."

CHALLENGE carried out a few towing jobs for the Navy control before setting back under orders for Dover harbour.

"On our way back we found a damaged destroyer loaded with troops. We got a line to her and towed her back to port, where the troops were able to disembark safely."

s.b. *LUCY RICHMOND:*
The French site mentions s.b. *LADY RICHMOND*. There is no such barge on record, and we believe it should be *LUCY RICHMOND*. She was a boomie, built in 1875 according to Richard Smith, and described as a schooner of 128 tons in the Merchant Navy lists of 1938. She had been built in Ipswich, built by E.J Robertson at St. Peters Dockyard at Ipswich, who is was a barge builder from 1872. She was registered in Maldon by Charles Marshall of Faversham and by 1938 owned by T. Scholey, East Greenwich. We have found no other mention of her participation in the evacuation.

The waiting game

"The mornings were still, the sea like smoked glass, but there was oil in the water, a pall of fear and grief hung over us. The tragic stuff, I thought were the injured. The corpse's, well the dead have received absolution – those without limbs will suffer a lifetime of punishment. I still dream about it."

When entering Dunkirk waters for the first time the first vessel that the crew of the *CHALLENGE* observed was her sister-tug

CONTEST which was also crewed from Gravesend. Both tugs were unarmed.

Not all the barges that volunteered were sent to the beaches. Barges and most small boats had to be towed across. The tugs were working non stop for days and logistically couldn't take them all. Besides, many of the Thames barges that went to Dunkirk were to be beached and abandoned. It was vital for some to be reserved for essential work at home.

Chris Barnes:
"I know what it is to feel hungry, outside closets, back to back houses. My dad was a miner, he died when I was 2 years old, I think it was either a pit accident or lung disease, my mum died of cancer when I was 9. I was brought up by my grandparents. I remember stoking that blasted stove that smoked like b****ry. There were no bathrooms, my grandfather came home covered with coal dust. My grandmother heated up water on the black stove to fill a tin bath by the fire for him. Once a week I went in after him. In 1926, when the mine owners decided to cut miner's wages and at the same time increase their working hours, there was a General Strike. Life was very hard in mining villages. Women and children were literally starving. Grandfather took me to "the Hirings" at Whitehaven when I was 14. I stood against a post at the fair, not an amusement fair you understand, a fair for the sale of animals, sheep, horses, cows, pigs, and waited for someone to pick you out. I went back to the Hirings and got another similar 'indenture' when that finished but I couldn't find another job. I was too old at16. After a couple of weeks Grandfather told me 'I can't afford to keep you, I'll have to take you down the mine.' Some of the seams in those Cumbrian mines go right out under the sea. I would have had to hew coal. I knew about pit disasters so I made up my mind I wasn't going to do that.

"I arrived in London with a penny halfpenny in my pocket. I got a job, got married and had a little girl and then I was called up. I had been on the switchboard at an hotel in London, so that qualified me for the Royal Corps of Signals, they said, and they sent me to France.

"They (the Germans) had taken over Austria, Czechoslovakia, Romania, Holland, Belgium, France. England was next. They were invincible, we were on the run and my wife and kiddie were in Hastings, right in their way. Who would look after them?"

Men were arriving at the beaches in a terrible state. They often had no water for two days, and no food for longer. They had seen trains bombed, pieces of cattle and people raining down on them, cattle trucks full of terrified refugees, women and children. If the Germans came to Britain they knew what we were in for.

British troops evacuating Dunkirk's beaches. Many stood shoulder deep in the sea for hours, to board the waiting naval vessels [2]

The Luftwaffe, that fighting force which included Germany's finest gentlemen strafed refugee columns almost as though it was target practice.

At 10.35am on 31st May Vice Admiral Wake Walker reported the conditions off the beach were very bad owing to a freshening on shore breeze. Tired men not used to working off a beach were finding it almost impossible to push away the boats heavy with men, which were being blown back onto or on top of them.

Rescued British troops gathered in a ship at Dunkirk [2]

a.b. *THYRA:*
THYRA was built by Albert A. Hutson of Maidstone in 1913, 70 tons, registered in Rochester No. 127262 and by 1934, like *PUDGE*, was owned by LRTC. Many of their vessels were river barges and were not required to register with the board of trade. The company paid better wages than other owners, but for some of the crews, the work was boring crossing maybe three times a week from Gravesend to Tilbury and back again. She now had an engine and carried 63 tons. Brought from Tilbury to Dover by *SUN XII* along with sailing barges *ROYALTY, H.A.C.* and *BEATRICE MAUD* her Skipper E. Filley took her to Dunkirk, towed by the tug *ST. ABBS.*

It was 5am on 1st June by the time *ST. ABBS* arrived with her and s.b. *H.A.C.*, casting them both off and returning to other duties. *THYRA* towed *H.A.C.* on to the beach. There was fierce bombing and the bargemen, with no battledress, no steel helmets or any other protection were in the thick of it. The carried on, working their hulls with the tide up the sandy beach near to *GLENWAY* and *LARK*. The idea had been that the French would unload the stores from the barges after the tide had ebbed but before it could be done the crews were ordered out. The bombing and machine gunning was now unremitting.

Skipper Filley:
  "We got eleven French soldiers off to our barge, others refused to come as they wanted to stay in France, not come to England."

Skipper Filley recorded that during the nine grilling hours he expected every moment to be his last, but he got all the other crews together with their soldiers on to *THYRA*, which, while laying on the shoreline from 5am to 2pm seemed to be the selected target for the Nazis. Eventually R.A.F. fighters drove them away, shooting four of them down. *THYRA* was never hit during that raid.

During the return voyage the Nazi 'planes continued to try to sink anything and everything that floated and some of the bombs falling close by her lifted her out of the water. By the time she returned to home shores, towed by the tug *EMPIRE HENCHMAN*, her hull was splintered, her engine damaged and her bollards strained through so much difficult and dangerous towing. She was last seen at Poole, Dorset.

s.b. *GRETA:*
Built and registered in Harwich, in 1892, 46 tons, *GRETA* is the oldest active Dunkirk Little Ship. Built for a barge sail-maker called Edward Alfred Hibbs at Brightlingsea Essex by Stones,

length 80ft, displacement 49 tons. Her usual cargo consisted of grain, malt and building products. She did however carry some more unusual things for example the spars for the German Kaiser's racing schooner in 1918. She was sold by Perry to LRTC and early in World War II was chartered by the Ministry of Supply to carry ammunition from the army depot at Upnor, Kent to Royal Navy vessels anchored in the Thames Estuary.

She took part in the evacuation from Dunkirk in 1940. Her War service ended in 1946. After a thorough overhaul and having an engine fitted she returned to normal trading, carrying grain, timber and animal feed.

GRETA returned to Dunkirk for the 60th anniversary of the evacuation. It was a wonderful Millennium crossing with three veterans (Dick, Bert, and Sid) aboard recalling the memories of their trip across the English Channel in WWII. *GRETA* was one of the Dunkirk little ships to brave the crossing. Dick thought it was strange to get the picture from the Little Ships point of view as sixty years earlier he had been on the beaches, waiting in the water to be picked up.

After the trip Dick wrote sharing his thoughts on the day:
"Until now I had never seen it from the Little Ships point of view. I was a soldier on the beach. I, like thousands of others had no idea how long it had taken those frail craft to reach us. All I knew was that they were there and help was at hand. Now I was on one of those little ships that had actually taken part in the evacuation. I could feel the tension as we prepared to enter Dunkirk Harbour.
Slowly we edged our way through the lock gates where an amazing sight met our eyes. Dense crowds lined the water's edge, cheering, clapping, and shouting words of welcome. Ships were sounding their sirens, the noise was deafening. We three veterans, stood together on the bows of GRETA, we were the only ones to cross the channel on the Little Ships.

The crowd, seeing the medals glinting in the sunlight gave us a special greeting."

At the 2000 reunion of the Little Ships *GRETA's* Skipper Steven Norris spoke with Prince Charles while moored in Dunkirk harbour. The TV commentator clearly had no idea that Prince Charles would make this impromptu stop. You could hear papers being shuffled as he tried desperately to find out details of the vessel and the name of its skipper that Prince Charles was talking to, then of course he mis-pronounced *GRETA's* name. She was re-rigged in the early 1980's. *GRETA* also returned to Dunkirk for the 70th Anniversary in 2010 and was used by the BBC as a base for filming interviews for 'live' news during the crossing and in Dunkirk Harbour for the main & local BBC news broadcasts. *GRETA* is in 2012 owned by and is home to Steven Norris. She is moored at Standard Quay Faversham, available to charter.

s.b. BARBARA JEAN

The River Orwell and the Port of Ipswich have been trading since Roman times. The Saxons established busy routes to the continent in the 7th century. Canute sailed up the river to disembark at Ipswich in 1016; ships were built here for King Henry VIII to defeat the Spanish and during the war against Napoleon, to keep the French at bay. The most consistent contribution to the crown has also been the grain trade, aided by the wooden barges first employed here hundreds of years ago.

BARBARA JEAN turning up Gravesend reach in the 1930's with Charlie Webb snr. at the wheel [9]

In May 1940 Ipswich once again gave her ships to war service, among them five of Paul's barges. Two of the largest ever used on the Thames were two steel hulled barges built at Brightlingsea in 1924. *AIDIE* and *BARBARA JEAN* each carried a cargo of about 260 tons and were of 119 tons net weight.

A fine big craft, *BARBARA JEAN* was registered in Ipswich for R & J Paul of Ipswich, the largest barge in their fleet. The National Archive holds no official log or crew list, although when 'Old Charlie' left her on 17th May 1940 for *AUDREY* he was replaced by Charlie Webb 'Young Charlie', of 42, Long Street Ipswich, with his mate, J. English.

'Old' Charlie Webb [8]

'Young Charlie' Webb sailed Paul's barges for almost 50 years. He was born in 1900, joining the company in 1914 when still 13 years old as third hand or cook on *ENA*, which was skippered by his father Old Charlie. The cooking was plain grub. The first thing all lads learned was how to make a currant duff, made with flour, beef suet and a few currants mixed with water and tied up in a piece of cloth. The duff had to be placed in a saucepan of boiling water, topped up from time to time with more boiling water. Keith Webb learned the hard way when, being seasick on his first trip as third hand with his father on *HYDROGEN*, he lazily topped up with cold water and received a cuff around the head for his slimy offering. The duff was a staple food for most bargemen, had at least once a week, more if times were hard. 'Young Charlie' had sailed often unofficially with his own father during school holidays. His first command was *COLNE* in 1924, followed by *SERB*, and then *BARBARA JEAN* (named after Russell Paul's daughter), one of several sailing barges that belonged to Paul's, that crossed to Dunkirk in 1940 loaded with military stores and explosives, as well as water in cans for the stranded soldiers.

The job of the "Little Ships" was to ferry the stranded army out to the destroyers waiting offshore, but the sailing barges were cargo vessels and some were to take supplies of ammunition and water to the beach, and then be abandoned.

Charlie wrote an account of his life 'on the barges' as he put it, which he gave to Richard Smith, who passed it on to David Wood who kindly shared it with us:

'It was not a nice job during the war in small craft. (One trip)... I was bound home and thought I had time to take the ebb tide round the Gunfleet end and anchor in the Wallett before dark but was unlucky and had to keep under way after dark getting towards the Naze about midnight. I was seen by a Harwich trawler, found the navy aboard about three in the morning and was escorted into harbour, going 'on the carpet' in Harwich. I was told I was lucky not to be fired on and sunk.

After several more cargoes (of wheat or maize) I received orders from my firm R & W Paul of Ipswich to take their BARBARA JEAN light to London."

Ipswich port records show *BARBARA JEAN,* skipper Charlie Webb with Jo English as mate bound for London 25th May.

Jo English, mate on the BARBARA JEAN [8]

"... on arrival at Erith we were taken over for the evacuation of Dunkirk. We were towed to Gravesend the same night and went alongside Tilbury Jetty for degaussing owing to mines."

Most 20th C Vessels are like huge floating magnets with a large magnetic field surrounding them. Because of its distortion effects on the Earth's magnetic field, the ship can act as a trigger device for magnetic sensitive ordnance or devices which are designed to detect these distortions. The degaussing system is installed aboard ship to reduce the ship's effect on the Earth's magnetic field. In order to accomplish this, the change in the Earth's field about the ship's hull is "cancelled" by controlling the electric current flowing through degaussing coils wound in specific locations within the hull. This, in turn, reduces the possibility of detection by these magnetic sensitive ordnance or devices.

"We were then towed to Dover by a Sun tug and were asked if we would volunteer for the voyage or not. We had to guess where for, but most crews agreed and stopped aboard. I was then loaded with a cargo of about 150 tons of fresh water and stores, etc. We left Dover at 14.45 on 31st May in tow of a Sun tug, having been given an 'escort' to help us get rid of our cargo, six privates and a sergeant.

"There was plenty of fire and heat on arrival. My tug went full ahead when nearing the beach. We slipped the tow and ran the vessel right up on the beach. I asked for help to get the cargo ashore but I must say I got no reply to do the job from anybody. It was a terrible sight, more like daylight as shrapnel and bombs were dropping. I could see and hear our soldiers as ranks were hit on the sea wall. We were glad when daylight arrived but nobody came near us on the beach so we decided on that day's tide to get the barge off beach as (soon as) we floated and sail about Dunkirk roads waiting for orders.

"I expect it looked a bit funny a 200 ton barge sailing about. One German bomber was hit, looked like coming down right on board but it missed us by about ten feet and passed into the sea. I pulled our Union Jack down to half mast and a speedboat came from the pier-head and asked what the trouble was!

"I told them I only wanted some orders for my vessel and could I could take her back to England as we were doing no good here. They came back with orders to beach her again and get out of the ship as the Germans were getting very near. I then signed the order releasing my six privates and sergeant and our luck held with several near hits but we got them aboard a large trawler.

"I was given my last warning by the Master of the trawler and got told to get away as soon as possible. I then sailed the barge onto the beach again letting go anchor and thirty fathoms of chain. I had to leave nearly all I had aboard and take to our boat. My mate Jo and the cook rowed us off to sea about two miles where we boarded a trawler but our troubles were not over by a long way as the trawler master got close to the beach and we were left high and dry for four hours. The Germans tried hard to hit us but we floated in safety but were machine gunned halfway across the channel, near hits but our luck held and we were soon off Dover. We had to lay off in the channel for some time as the Germans were dropping mines".

"We landed at Dover but looked a bit rough for a London Sunday but our friends the Cockneys soon put that right and treated us like lords. We were given a snack of food and left Dover early on Sunday morning for home. I arrived home at tea time just as a nice feed was on the table, you can guess my wife and children were glad to see me, (we had at that time 4 boys and a girl).

I was fairly tired so after a good wash and feed I went to bed. We had several air raid warnings that night but they didn't bother me at all. I reported to the owners next morning and gave them ships papers about all I had saved. Then I had a day or two's holiday while I was waiting for a job as my firm had three barges left at Dunkirk, BARBARA JEAN, AIDIE and DORIS, with only ENA and TOLLESBURY coming back."

There are not many laughs in these stories but I do like the one Charlie Webb told his family who lived in Long Street, now demolished to make way for Suffolk College.

Every Paul's barge carried a pennant with her name when she was built. They were about 12 feet long, red, pointed, with the barge name in white.

Charlie's daughter Pam:

"I can see him now, walking up Long Street weeks later, filthy dirty with odd shoes on and carrying a flag under his arm. Among all the flak, dive bombing, noise and mayhem of the beach he had brought the flag home. 'Oi hed to leave me barge' he said 'but I'm d****d if I was gorn to let the b*****s hev the flag."

BARBARA JEAN was set on fire on the beach. [8]

Those old skippers thought more of their barges than they did their wives, so they say. Ena was one of Charlie's children named after a Paul's barge that had a similar flag, brought home from Dunkirk by *ENA*'s skipper Titch Page when he abandoned her on the beach.

Pam recalls:

"Charlie would never let anyone take the wheel, he was always in charge of his own barge. He couldn't swim – the number of times he was fished out of the river with a stick! He was taken to court once for taking home a bit of driftwood he got out of the river. If there was a bob or two to be made my dad and Uncle Harold (Smy) were there, you could bet on it."

£3,495 was paid to Pauls as compensation in 1941; she was later salvaged and served as a coal store in Dunkirk Harbour.

CHARLIE WEBB JNR

Charlie Webb in Ipswich with ENA as a motor barge, 1973 [8]

Charlie's grandson Gary:
"I used to think he was a giant, my grandad. I remember walking down Long Street when I was only little, holding my grandad's hand. He had a bit of rope round his trousers to hold them up, so I had to have one too, to be like him. I spent my holidays on ENA when he had her".

Pam later had a fruit and vegetable shop next to Clarke's the ships chandlers and butchers on the corner of Tacket Street in Ipswich. Other Webb bargemen include Keith, mate to Charlie before the war and subsequently skipper of *ORINOCO*, Reuben, skipper of *TRILBY,* and Alby, skipper of *RAYBELL.*

After about three days without a job 'Young Charlie' was given the sailing barge *AUDREY*. Six months later she was hit by a collier almost cutting her in half. He was out of work again, as was his brother-in-law Harold when his barge, the *BIJOU* caught fire at Mistley during an air raid and was burnt out at the water's edge.

> *"I could not see my children without enough food as Paul's wages on the yard were very low in 1941. We thought we would try the sugar beet factory at Bramford. My wages were about £8 a week so it was better than going to sea. In BARBARA JEAN my wages had been £4.10.0 a week."*

But barging was in his blood and 'Young Charlie' later became master of *THALATTA, JOCK, LADY JEAN, GRAVELINES* and *ENA*.

OUR BOYS ARE COMING HOME

Each one of us will try to imagine the thoughts and feelings of those men – and a few women. We can only imagine it through our own experience, picture it in our heads. But every man or woman on that beach was an individual. Each had their own priorities, hopes and fears. Some had very little imagining, just did as they were told, kept their heads down 'ploughing a straight furrow' as had been their experience in another life. Some were educated men who had had great expectations. Some had loved, some had lost love, and some had never known it.

Provost Jetties [2]

At low tide vehicles were driven into the sea to construct a 'Provost Jetty' so that at high tide larger ships could get closer to the beaches. It would have been a precarious journey for a man to attempt, jumping from one to the other, and another cause of accidents, with men lost.

Burning oil tanks were beacons for the rescuers from England to follow, a sinister signal seen by those waiting in Dover. The billowing clouds of smoke covered the beaches so that mercifully waves of dive bombers returned to base, not finding their targets.

Douglas Bader, a member of 222 Squadron, stationed at Martlesham Heath aerodrome in Suffolk attempted to protect Allied forces leaving Dunkirk. Bader had lost both legs in a flying accident 7 years earlier, but was *the* flying ace of the Royal Air Force. He became an icon, exemplifying the creed 'The British never give up'.

Bader:
"We were all flying around up and down the coast near Dunkirk looking for enemy aircraft which seemed also to be milling around with no particular cohesion. The sea from Dunkirk to Dover during these days of the evacuation looked like any coastal road in England on a bank holiday. It was solid with shipping. One felt one could walk across without getting one's feet wet, or that's what it looked like from the air. There were naval escort vessels, sailing dinghies, rowing boats, paddle-steamers, indeed every floating device known in this country. They were all taking British soldiers from Dunkirk back home. The oil-tanks just inside the harbour were ablaze, and you could identify Dunkirk from the Thames estuary by the huge pall of black smoke rising straight up in a windless sky. Our ships were being bombed by enemy aeroplanes up to about half-way across the Channel and the troops on the beaches were suffering the same attention. There were also German aircraft inland strafing the remnants of the British Expeditionary Force fighting their way out to the port." (Martlesham Heath Aviation Society)

Although the Luftwaffe repeatedly bombed and strafed the ships and men waiting to board them the intensity of aerial activity meant that the tanks had to be kept out of the fray in order that

Göering could show off the prowess of his air force. There were overhead clouds and misty mornings, preventing the Luftwaffe keeping up their attacks. Although on 27th May, 29th and 1st June they inflicted terrible losses of men and ships, for the most part the weather prevented follow up.

Until now there had been a light breeze from the southwest, later from the east, instead of the northerlies which had been expected. The freshening on-shore breeze on 31st May presented a problem, blowing the small boats back into the sand and surf as they tried to get off. Only on 5th June after the evacuation, did a stiff northerly wind blow great breakers, normal for this coast.

> *"I can't swim. Lots of us blokes couldn't. It was a bit hairy standing up to your neck in water as you queued for your turn to be picked up, but I didn't see any panic. Enemy planes were flying overhead especially during the day but there was so much smoke from things burning, not only from the town but one really crummy thing, some of the boats abandoned on the beach, or vehicles our boys set on fire so the enemy couldn't use them, that the Germans couldn't see us so they fired at random. Thank God some of the shells were duds. At Dover the organisation was great. As soon as we got ashore there were cups of tea and sandwiches, there were trains laid on to get us away as soon as possible and when we arrived in London there was more tea and sandwiches."*

s.b. *ETHEL MAUD:*
ETHEL MAUD, a barge 80ft 2ins long with a displacement of 57 tons, was built by Howard's of Maldon of pitch pine on oak in 1889 for James Keeble of Maldon. She was sold to Parkers and then Green Brothers, the Maldon millers. Her type was known as a stack barge or 'stackie'. Stackies were loaded with hay and straw from the farms of Essex, Kent and Suffolk, to feed and bed the working horses on the streets of East London.

Their appearance when loaded also earned them the name of 'haystack barges' and they frequently returned with cargoes of 'scrapings' - horse manure swept from the streets of the City and put to good use by the farmers of East Anglia. They carried a variety of cargoes which were quicker and cheaper to transport by barge than by horse-drawn wagon or even by the early railways. When Tilbury docks opened in 1958, the old traffic to the docks of London diminished and the working boats gradually lost their importance.

Despite her age, *ETHEL MAUD* was fast, her moveable bowsprit carrying two staysails, a jib and a foresail. She had a mainsail, topsail and mizzen and could, on occasion, add two more foresails used like spinnakers. Barge rig allows for spars to be lowered easily to pass under bridges and despite a three-foot draft, lee-boards gave them an improved performance to windward.

She crossed to Dunkirk with supplies and stores for the BEF, and is on the National Register of Historic Ships. Later she was fitted with a BMC 56hp Diesel engine. *ETHEL MAUD* was finally sold into retirement in 1963. She is now a houseboat at Rochester.

s.b. *ROYALTY:*
Everard and Sons of Greenhithe commissioned *ROYALTY,* 85tons, in 1898.

Captain Henry Miller, BEM. from *'Dick the Dagger'*:
"We was at Greenhithe. I had the ROYALTY then laying off waiting for orders. Mr. Everard called me ashore and told me they were going to take us to Ramsgate. We thought we were going to unload a ship sunk on the Goodwins and we were going to lighten her. Anyhow, the tug came for us, one of Alexander's Sun Tugs from Gravesend, took us to Southend that night."
The log book of *SUN XII* records that she left Tilbury Docks at 23:00 on 29th May 1940 for Ramsgate towing the a.b. *THYRA* and

sailing barges *ROYALTY*, *H.A.C* and *BEATRICE MAUD*. She was then ordered on to Dover, arriving there at 15:00 next day.

Captain Millar continues:
> "Next day we towed to Ramsgate with the TOLLESBURY and then went to Dover: laid in there two or three days. There was a lot of barges in there, they was all loading cargoes. ETHEL EVERARD, (and) AIDIE, BARBARA JEAN, both Pauls of Ipswich, they were loading. We were one of the last to load. Then they told us the tug CERVIA would be taking us out of the dock, destination unknown: 'Captain of the tug would have your orders'. We had a rough guess when we was loaded where we was going. So they towed us all across the channel towards Dunkirk".

The tug *CERVIA*, Master Capt W H Simmons, left Dover at 21:40 on 31st May with *ROYALTY* in tow, loaded with food, water and ammunition. She carried six soldiers who were to help unload the cargo.

In company was the tug *PERSIA* towing two dumb lighters *SARK* and *SHETLAND*. They arrived 1 mile east of Dunkirk pier at 07:20 on 1st June. Her skipper Henry Miller (Dick the Dagger), with Mate Ernie Coe, Third hand Ernie Miller aimed to set her as far up the sands as possible so that the waiting, desperate troops could unload her as soon as the tide turned. They made ready for beaching, setting up the topsail to carry out this operation when a large number of German planes appeared overhead and immediately started bombing and machine gunning them. *ROYALTY,* being towed at full speed, slipped her tow, set her topsail and beached herself head on to Malo beach. They let go the anchor when they reached the beach, still being attacked, the decks continually sprayed with bullets.

Miller:
> "We were told to put the barge ashore and the soldiers would unload us. We had food, cans of water and ammunition; yes

live shells and all the cargo was below hatches, none on deck. They (the German army and the Luftwaffe) had already started firing and shelling right along the sand. All the soldiers had gone off the sand and gone onto the jetty, we put ROYALTY ashore and only half an hour later a French officer come in a pinnace and told us 'Get out of her we are going to blow her up. (There were lots of barges) All of them other were ashore. The tide was coming in and I had put her (ROYALTY) ashore where I could. I was worried about these here 'planes gunning us and the bullets going right through the hatches and hitting the shells stacked in the hold."

Since no one came along to unload the stores Miller ordered the barge boat put down and the crew and the six soldiers rowed off to the tug *CERVIA*.

"Soon as he told us to get out of her we got in the boat and rowed off to the tug. He was awaiting for us out there, All the other crews had gone off the barges. We were not near them, couple of miles up the beach at Malo Les Bains.

"The mate (Kenny Coe), my son Ernie who was third hand and some soldiers who had come aboard at Dover. They was to help unload so we was all in the barge boat rowing out to the tug when there come a Jerry 'plane, dropped a couple of bombs, missed then come back and machine gunned us. Missed again. It was a bit hot I can tell you. They bombed and sunk two destroyers while we was there, direct hits. We got out to the tug and the skipper said 'We cannot do any good here so we come back down and we saw the barge TOLLESBURY at anchor. We went alongside. We got on the barge and found about 150 soldiers down in her hold. There was no wind so she was not going anywhere so we passed her tow rope over to the tug. We broke the windlass getting the anchor free then we started towing to Ramsgate. During our trip back we picked up a lifeboat from the Orient Liner ORION loaded with about 25 soldiers. Some had been shot up

pretty badly. The boat's engine had broken-down and no-one knew how to fix it.

"Us bargemen all volunteered to go over you know. When they got us together at Dover we didn't know where we were going to exactly, and some of the poor devils never came back. Mr. Everard told me I had to go to the palace on so-and-so day. So me and my son went up, shook hands with the King, had a chat about Dunkirk, pinned on my medal and said 'Well done skipper'.

"I carried on barging right through the war. My mate Kenny Coe a young Greenhithe man, left the barges and went on one of Everards motor-ships, the ADAPTITY. He lost his life on 5th October 1940 when she struck a mine off Harwich."

A handwritten report by Master of the tug *CERVIA*, Captain Simmons,:

"Friday 31st May Left Dover 9pm towing Sailing Barge ROYALTY loaded with provisions, cans of fresh water and cigarettes for the troops stranded on Dunkirk beaches. We had orders to beach the ROYALTY at Port Malo about one mile east of Dunkirk pier heads. We passed through the downs at midnight.

The tide was ebbing as we towed up through the Roads but progress was slow as we had to keep easing down on account of the H.M. Destroyers and Channel Packets wash as they steamed out in a constant procession in and away from Dunkirk Harbour. Outward bound full of troops. Troops everywhere on board them. The great evacuation was on. There were a great number of wrecks about and great caution was necessary as few were charted or buoyed. The only means of knowing where they were apart from any wreckage visible above water was the tide rip over them. We passed Dunkirk pier-heads where five H.M Destroyers were loading up with troops and we passed two big French Destroyers that had been mined and were lying wrecked up on the beach. We shot our barge off toward the beach at 8.20am.

"Soldiers were running down the beach to meet her when an air raid siren began to blow ashore and the soldiers took what cover they could find.

We dropped our anchor at 08.20 all being quiet when over came about 15 enemy planes with guns firing away on shore at them. Two Destroyers and a Sloop outside of us us began to open fire as the planes began to bomb them and as the Destroyers were twisting and turning at high speed to dodge the bombs I deemed it necessary to keep out of their way so hove up anchor and paddled in towards the shore, our own Lewis gun firing at the planes as they came over us.

"At this time our barge's boat was rowing off to us, with six soldier stevedores also the Master and Mate of the ROYALTY which was now beached and anchored on the shore. Two more barge crews rowed to us in one boat and we took them all on board. One of them was DUCHESS.

The destroyer outside of us had a stick of bombs (9) dropped in the water alongside of her. They exploded underwater as she kept her speed twisting and turning to dodge them. She must have been holed as she began to take a list and was getting deeper by the head.

"(We) Began to run off to her the guns firing all the time at the planes. On my way I saw a white motor lifeboat drifting with about 15 soldiers in it. I picked her up transferring the soldiers to us and leaving the lifeboat astern with the other two small boats. The destroyer proved to be H.M.S KEITH.

"I had to keep clear of her as the sloop was circling her at high speed in an attempt to fight off the raiders. I saw one plane brought down in a cloud of smoke just west of the pierheads, also another destroyer that was hit by a bomb.

At 08:00 the destroyer *KEITH* began to list and was again bombed; her guns were going all the time as she steamed round and round. The tug *VINCIA* began to pick up survivors and the tug *ST. ABBS* came alongside the *KEITH*'s starboard bow. A sloop also went to her assistance. At 08:15 the Royal Naval destroyer *IVANHOE* to the westward was seen to be disabled and a small tanker the mine sweeper *SKIPJACK* astern of the *VINCIA* went up in flames.

H.M.S. KEITH in 1937 [+]

Captain Simmons:
> *The big tug ST ABBS was making her way to H.M.S KEITH and by this time the KEITH had dropped her anchor and swung to the flood tide. Another tug which proved to be our VINCIA was running down the roads from the eastward. The planes were still bombing the KEITH trying for her depth charges but her guns failed to answer this time as the crew had been ordered to abandon her and they were dropping into the sea on rafts and spars and one or two boats, but a lot were swimming away from her on the tide and the enemy planes made another dive at them machine gunning the men in the water. As they drove up away from their ship the VINCIA began to pick them up and I turned round and began to run down the roads towards the other disabled destroyer. The tug ST. ABBS had got alongside the KEITH just as a direct hit by an enemy plane exploded the depth charges on her stern and blew the destroyers stern right off and I later*

heard that the ST ABBS was sunk by a direct hit alongside the KEITH. I saw a sloop hit by a bomb just north of the tug VINCIA and the next second a ball of fire and smoke was a thousand feet above her. I later heard this was H.M.S. SKIPJACK taking ammo to the troops at Dunkirk. Halfway to the entrance to the harbour I saw a sailing barge at anchor with a lot of soldiers about her decks. I went alongside of her and told them to come on board and we would leave the barge where she was but I was told by an Army Captain that there was 250 including many badly wounded soldiers down in the hold, covered, so that enemy planes would not spot them. I put a towing spring on her bow but in a swell from a passing Sloop, rope jerked the wooden winch from its bed and would then not heave so began towing the barge with at least 15 fathom of chain out attached to her anchor. She was the coasting barge TOLLESBURY.

The wail of that siren ushered in the attack which, had it been made earlier, might have been decisive in the history of Dunkirk. This devastating raid appeared to be synchronised with the first German assault of the day on the perimeter line. A very heavy force of enemy bombers attacked; predominately Junkers dive bombers re-enforced by twin-engine Junkers 88s, elaborately escorted by fighters.

The destroyers were short of ammunition, having fought against attack continuously for days and had little or no time to receive further ammunition during their short spells in Dover, simply taking on oil and returning to lay off the beaches. There were no allied aircraft in the skies above, no escort for the ships. The attack on the nearest ships was awesome. From allied forces behind the beaches, from the harbour, from the few ships which had firepower, came a response. The sky was filled with exploding shells, the lines of tracer bullets and the whistle and roar of projectiles. The sea was flecked with small plumes as the splinters of the shells whistled into the water and all around the huge, dramatic fountains from the bombs that dropped relentlessly.

CERVIA's master continued his account:
"A British destroyer outside of us began to fire at the enemy planes and bombs began to fall near her as she steamed about. At full speed with her helm hard to port nine bombs fell in a line in the water along her starboard side and they exploded under water heeling the destroyer over on her beam ends, but she was righted again and a sloop joined in the gunfire, also shore batteries and as they made off towards the land they machine-gunned us and we returned the fire with our Lewis gun."

CERVIA then took in tow s.b. *TOLLESBURY* which had 200 troops under the hatches. The M.L.B. *ORIENT IV* was added to the tow and *CERVIA* proceeded down Dunkirk roads. When west of the pier heads, *IVANHOE* was seen to be in tow of the *PERSIA* and *VINCIA* with decks full of survivors as they passed.

At 09:00, whilst at No 5 W Buoy about 20 planes appeared. *IVANHOE* put up a smoke screen and 9 bombs fell near a cross channel boat which however kept going. Five bombs fell about 100 feet off *CERVIA*'S port bow lifting the tug out of the water. A bomb exploded between a sloop and the disabled destroyer she was towing. Mine sweeper *SALTASH* was seen towing the destroyer HMS *HAVANT*.

At last tug *CERVIA* made for home, with the crew from s.b *ROYALTY* aboard, and the 25 soldiers, as well as the crew of s.b. *DUCHESS*, the crew of the *ORIENT IV* and towing s.b. *TOLLESBURY*. They were in the Downs by 15:00. With these and subsequent actions *CERVIA* brought about 230 troops out of Dunkirk, They arrived at Gravesend at 09:30 on 2nd June.

It had been decided earlier that day that Commander-in-Chief BEF General Gort should board *KEITH*. Wake-Walker had planned that Gort would leave his villa at about 06:00. Once on the beach west of La Panne they would be picked up and taken to the destroyer by a naval launch. In the event the plan became confused and while his staff were taken to *KEITH*, Gort himself went aboard the minesweeper *HEBE*, to be reunited with his staff just after midnight on 1st June. He and Brigadier Leese then boarded a speedboat, and made for Dover, arriving safely at 06:20. Wake-Walker at last could breathe. He had managed the recovery of the Commander-in Chief of the BEF - losing him to an enemy attack or capture had been his worst nightmare, and the potential loss had been only too close.

Tug *ST ABBS*, one of the saint class built Ferguson Shipbuilders. Ltd. (Port Glasgow, Scotland) was lost later on the 1st June (or early on 2nd) with the survivors still on board. One hundred navy and army personnel were lost in the tug. Her Master Lt. T. Brooker RN had come out of retirement to volunteer for the operation.

TWO TINS OF BISCUITS AND FIVE CANS OF WATER

Five of R & W Paul's barges took part in the evacuation, *TOLLESBURY, ENA, BARBARA JEAN, AIDIE* and *DORIS*.

TOLLESBURY is a wooden barge built in 1901 by H. Felton, at Sandwich, as a cargo vessel. Official Number: 110315. Length Overall 84ft, displacement 70tons. She was named by Mr. Fisher, her owner in 1901 from the fishing village of Tollesbury in Essex, on a tributary of the river Blackwater. The village was a loading port for the stack barges which could lie alongside for horse drawn wagons to unload them.

TOLLESBURY entering Ipswich docks through the lock, 1920's *

From 1912 she joined the fleet of R & W Paul Ltd, of East Anglia, maltsters, purchased for £500. She carried mostly grain, malt and animal feeds but also stone, coal, coke and pitch around the south coast and across the channel.

Roger Finch:
"The organisers of 'Operation Dynamo' were especially anxious to enrol wooden sailing barges in the rescue attempt, for they could run up the gently shelving Dunkirk beach,

immune from magnetic and acoustic mines, and act as embarking points for the troops who, using them as a bridge, could then reach the safety of deeper draught rescue vessels."

Ipswich Port records show *TOLLESBURY* departing 26th May; skipper Lemon Webb (Lem). Next day, Lem with his mate Edward 'Gunner' Gunn and third hand 'Scotty' Scott, (of 13, Kemp Street, Ipswich) were sailing *TOLLESBURY* up the Thames near Erith when a naval launch came alongside. The Port of London official ordered him to go instead to Cory's jetty at Sheerness. There, he, the mate Gunner and a young lad, nineteen, were given the choice to leave the ship or to volunteer to evacuate the BEF from Dunkirk. None of them hesitated. From there she was towed to Tilbury Basin and on to Dover with skipper, mate and third hand onboard.

On 31st May *SUN XII*, (owners: W H J Alexander and Co Ltd), with no recorded Naval Officer on board left Dover for Dunkirk at 16:00 under tug master A. V. Mee and navigator B. R. Mastin. The tug *SUN XII* towed both the big Everard barge *ETHEL EVERARD* loaded with shells, small arms ammunition, water and provisions for Dunkirk and *TOLLESBURY* loaded with stores and dynamite. Just making that dangerous journey with such a cargo, under heavy attack from the air, knowing that any direct hit would blow the vessel and its crew to smithereens would be enough to unnerve the bravest of souls. The tug *FAIRPLAY I* was also towing barges in company.

There was an air attack en route and by the time *TOLLESBURY* arrived, the light was fading. They arrived at Dunkirk at 23:50, both tugs putting their barges ashore at Bray-Dunes. The tow rope was dropped as far inshore as the tug's deep draught would allow. The three man crew were left to get on with it. Lem's orders were to beach, but as there was no wind at all, using the barge's long sweeps, the crew of three actually rowed her in the direction of the shore.

The calm night sea of summer was full of phosphorescence, so when an enemy aircraft approached the rowing had to stop so as not to give away their position. The sky was lit up by explosions or the eerie light of flares. Cries for help came from the shore as waiting troops sighted them.

Lem, his mate and the third hand got the soldiers to help them discharge the cargo and once done they were ordered to abandon *TOLLESBURY* for use as an embarkation platform to enable troops to reach the ships anchored in deeper water. At that moment Lem Webb displayed the most extraordinary courage. A barge man is a different fellow from a naval officer. He is an independent so-and-so, used to making his own decisions about the vessel in his charge. He was no less captain of his ship than those who commanded the destroyers and frigates lying off shore. He could, and did, disobey orders.

As he looked at the desperate men wading out towards him, their eyes full of hope, he said to himself 'B***** that'. He stood on his 84 feet of solid English Oak and decided he would not abandon her, or the men she could bring home. He lowered the heavy boarding ladder; a surge caused it to break against the hull. He and the mate swung the barge boat from the davits, lowering it so that the stern was level with the water. He then improvised a gangplank and waved the men to come aboard. Other men frantically clambered or were pulled up the leeboards and over the rail, sliding down into the illusory safety of the hold where they stood as one solid body in the darkness. Some were sea sick, some relieved themselves against the inwales; the barge smelled like a sewer and would have to be hosed and bilges pumped out before she could ever take another cargo of grain for Paul's. Under constant attack from the air, the barge was a sitting target as they waited anxiously for her to float, expecting at any moment to be hit.

Full as she could be, push as they might with the setting booms both the soldiers and crew could not get her clear of the shingle beach. As another day dawned, with the threat of more air attacks, then she lifted to the swell, carrying 273 soldiers off the beaches. Setting all sail Lem tacked further out before the wind dropped and he was forced to anchor. A signaller from among the soldiers fixed up two semaphore flags using broom handles and code flags. A destroyer, realising her plight, dashed to the rescue, preparing to take the soldiers off, but as a second destroyer came to the other side of the barge further air attacks forced them to move away. Both ships were sunk, but astonishingly *TOLLESBURY* was not hit.

Captain Simmons report continues to recount the events of the crossing until they anchored in the Old Cudd Channel:

"Motor boats then disembarked our troops, also took off the wounded out of the barge TOLLESBURY which could not be taken into the harbour on account of the congestion in there. In all about 270 soldiers were landed from us and from our tow. We were ordered to take the barge to Gravesend.

I enquired as to what had become of a fleet of 30 French and Belgium fishermen who had spoken to me early that morning on my way to Dunkirk, who were sailing with all their families to England. I had given them a course and wished them luck. I was told that they had all arrived safely well loaded with families and troops after having sailed right over the Goodwin Sands on the High water. That was just one of the Miracles of the evacuation.

We proceeded at 6 am towing the barge TOLLESBURY, ORION 1V and two small boats. We had towed the TOLLESBURY across with 15 fathoms of chain out on her anchor, forgetting all about the magnetic mines. At 10 pm we dropped anchor at Southend.

Sunday 2nd June: Proceeded at daylight for Gravesend. Made barge TOLLESBURY fast at the Ship and Lobster buoy and the ORION 1V and the two small boats I handed over to the Gravesend Customs."

Miraculously *TOLLESBURY* still was not damaged. On 1st June the tug *CERVIA* brought her safely home 100 miles to Blighty. Off the North Goodwin a mine exploded near her to starboard. Again she sustained no damage, finally dropping anchor in Ramsgate Roads.

A copy of a letter Charlie Webb's brother Lem wrote to his family afterwards thanks to Keith Webb, Charlie's son:
"11.6.1940
Dear Donald, Rhoda and Brian,
For a start I am getting on, the reaction is going off. I have been to the doctor today and got a tonic and sleeping dope, got sounded and is sound. I suppose you would like to know what we did.

"*We was commandeered at Erith, with eleven more, towed to Dover and then to Dunkirk, told to beach there. Before reaching there, miles off we could see the place burning, we all thought it was our last trip, the planes was over us all the way past the town, and one of our destroyers followed us firing at them until about 1 to 2 miles east of Dunkirk.*

"*The tug shot us off but we had not enough way to short on the beach so we got out the oars and rowed her on. We had to stop at times breaking water as planes came over and the water was like fire.*

"*A French battery was close and they took up firing protection, the soldiers was shouting barge, barge, frantic to get aboard, they waded in up to armpits to meet us.*

"*I dropped leeboards to hold her, it was calm, we put the ladders over but the cabin one broke, then we lowered the* boat for them, and as they got in I and my cook was pulling them up over the rails, it was a job to get their knees up on the gunwale with all their gear on. Gunner was doing his bit with the ladder.

"When the hold was full and the forecastle, the officers had (the) cabin, Brigadier, General, Captain and was full up. We daren't have them on deck to show off to the planes.
"We tried to get off but her stern held her and we laid there until six o'clock before floating. We pushed her off with the booms and set sails and tried to sail up and away, but wind was light, also tide against us, but we got off to a Belgium ship and she wirelessed for a tug. Then we had to anchor.

"Gunner morsed with flags to our destroyers, and one was fast coming alongside to get men off, when scores of jerries came over and our ships both sides let go all their guns at them. The planes nearly touched us, they raced off full speed circling round us. Firing also shore batteries. They made dives at us dropping bombs just clear. We had about four hours of that altogether as they kept coming at us, until we was nearly half way back to England.

"A tug happened to bring another barge over in the midst of the battle, and as soon as she was beached the crew got on the tug and she came and got us and towed us to Ramsgate where we put men ashore in motor boats.

"The tug put wire on our bit-head when getting us, you can bet we was all in a hurry to be gone, and pulled the bit-head over breaking the windlass, so we towed home anchor about too fins under her. This was all on Saturday, and we got to Southend dark that night.

"Hadn't had any sleep since Thursday night. Sunday morning we got to Gravesend and moored up to buoy there. It was

Sunday. I didn't know how to get Mum. I turned in till the afternoon and wrote home and went to post it after tea. Then I suddenly thought of you and you know the result.

"*I hadn't shaken a finger and was cool through it all, until I picked up the phone then I went all to pieces.*
"*I came home Thursday they sent relief captain from Ipswich and the barge got here today. My crew were grand men; they did everything without a murmur. The DORIS, ADIE and BARBARA JEAN are all lost over there. We are the only one (of Paul's barges) that brought back men that I know of. The crews of all the others are home. Goodbye for now.*
Dad. Thank you Brian.

As they brought them home Lemon Webb and his two man crew were able to give the 273 men aboard water from the cans loaded at Dover, two tins of biscuits and five cans of water.

Rescued troops aboard a barge approaching Dover

The Paul's barges that were lost were crewed by Lem's friends and colleagues. He must have been fearful for them, as well as trying to recover from such a terrible experience.

Ted Gunner became skipper of, among others, *ANGLIA*. Ipswich Port records show *TOLLESBURY* returning to Ipswich on 11th June. After the war Ernie Westwood left school at 14 years old to become cook/third hand/dogsbody on her. Later he worked with Gunner. He married the sister of Joseph English, the mate of *BARBARA JEAN*. Ernie's son David Westwood 'Wes' is now skipper of *VICTOR*. Barging was then, as now, a surprisingly small world.

The Port of London Authority report of July 1940 says:
"The Captain says the crew, a mate of 40 and a cook of 19, were marvellous, doing everything in their power to handle the barge and assist soldiers who were waist deep in the water, aboard".

TOLLESBURY continued in trade under sail. Her first engine was installed in 1950. She was taken out of trade in 1965, and then sailed privately. In 1978 she was a houseboat at Pin Mill on the River Orwell, owned by Mrs. D. Tonkin. She was rebuilt at Ipswich Dock-end in1989/1992 and powered by a Ruston and Honsby engine. She moved to London, owned by David Paling as a floating pub at Millwall. She was badly damaged by the IRA Docklands bomb in 1996 after which she was again restored. Having been put up for sale in 2004 she sunk at her berth in September 2005. She was raised and laid up at Fresh Wharf Estate, Barking Creek as a houseboat in 2010. She is registered with National Historic Ships UK.

WIN SOME – LOSE SOME

ETHEL EVERARD abandoned [II]

The largest spritsail barges were the four built for F. T. Everard and sons of Great Tower Street, Greenhithe, London. *ETHEL EVERARD* was a later barge, built in 1926 of iron, at the yard of Fellowes & Co. at Great Yarmouth for Everards, one of four, including the *WILL, ALF* and *FRED EVERARD*. She was registered in London, her owner as William J. Everard, Gravesend. From truck to keel she measured 112 feet (compare this to the 86 feet of *PUDGE*). She carried an amazing 158 tons, the largest of any other barge. The Everards had the biggest sail plan of all spritsail barges, measuring 112 ft. from deck to topmast truck, sprits of 65 feet. She set 5,600 sq. ft. of canvas, exclusive of the staysail. Originally using a crew of four hands, Skipper, mate and two boys, they later used only three, finding that one strong experienced man is more useful than two inexperienced boys.

ETHEL EVERARD 'Soldiers of the West Front! Dunkirk has fallen –with it has ended the greatest battle in world history' Copyright Adolph Hitler [II]

ETHEL EVERARD was towed to Dunkirk in company with *TOLLESBURY* by the tug *SUN XII* on 31st May. She was loaded with a dangerous cargo of shells and small arms ammunition as well as water and provisions. At the time it was hoped that the troops could make a stand, or at least buy precious time. Arriving at 11.30 that night she endured long hours of machine gunning and bombing all around her. The orders received by skipper T. Willis were to beach her so she slipped her tow about a mile east of Dunkirk piers, proceeding under sail until she touched ground, the tide taking her and swinging her broadside on. Not surprisingly the desperate troops waiting for rescue; imagined her to be their salvation and waded out, boarding her. She had a sergeant and five soldiers aboard to organise the unloading of the cargo. Thinking the oncoming soldiers had the same purpose they readily hailed them, only to discover that they were in fact among the thousands hoping to be evacuated. The huge steel *ETHEL EVERARD,* resting on the sand looked a safe haven. Even more immediate was their raging thirst.

"*Where do you keep the drinking water, Captain*"?

Thankfully a naval cutter from a nearby gunboat came to fetch them off. The sergeant and his men, together with all the barge crews, were taken off little more than an hour later by a naval gunboat.

"*You'll have to abandon them*" all the barge crews were told,
"*We are going to set your craft on fire.*"

Before setting off for Dover the gunboat shot down six of the host of planes circling round above. It must have offered little consolation to those brave men who lost their precious barges only to see the vital cargo they had risked their lives to deliver sent up in flames.

Photograph of the charred wreck of ETHEL EVERARD with triumphant German soldiers standing in front of her, used as propaganda saying this is what happens to the British Navy when it tangles with the Nazis. (Newbury Diesel Company)

The barge-yacht NANCIBELLE:
Unusually, the *NANCIBELLE* was a spritsail rigged schooner barge, her main mast stepped above the coach roof. She was designed by H.W. Harvey and was built by the Sittingbourne Ship Building Company, Kent in 1930. Her sails were by Putwayne. Her Official Number was 161498 and she measured 40.0 x 11.4 x 4.9 feet. By the start of WWII she had been fitted with a 2-cylinder Thoreycroft petrol engine. She helped in the evacuation of Dunkirk and she is credited with bringing back ninety-seven troops in a single voyage. *NANCIBELLE* now lies partially sunk on Church Beach, Penryn.

d.b. *SARK* and d.b. *SHETLAND*, a.b. *GLENWAY*:
Tug *PERSIA*, Owners: William Watkins Ltd. Tug Master: H Aldrich. Her logs detail that she left Dover on 29th May towing dumb barges *SARK* and *SHETLAND*. En route to Dunkirk, the tow parted twice.

30th May 1940 05.00 Anchored 4 miles east of Dunkirk
12.45 towed the barges to the East Pier head and anchored them as ordered
16.00 Left Dunkirk with soldiers & equipment.
23.59 Anchored in the Downs, disembarked troops 31st May

She immediately left Dover towing the barges *GLENWAY* and *LARK* in company with the tug *CERVIA* towing s.b *ROYALTY*. After discharging the barges at Dunkirk the crew saw the Royal Naval Destroyer *HMS IVANHOE* hit by a bomb. Following an order to take her in tow, they did so but the concussion from a bomb broke the towing hawser. They put another hawser on board and proceeded towards Dover. They were bombed for over two hours until British planes came and dispersed the enemy. *PERSIA* continued with her rescue work until 4th June at Dover. Although fired on by German shore batteries from the French coast, she suffered no damage. She brought home 27 troops.

*GLENWAY at Maldon
September 2002*

The last of the 'GLEN' barges, she was built by James Little at Borstal, Rochester, Kent in 1913, 82 tons, for Mr Hammond, later sold to John Wilks of Deal. In 1933 she was sold to Samuel West Ltd, of Gravesend, and she was fitted with a new engine the following year. Other Glen barges were *GLENDIVO*, 1901, *GLENMOVE*, 1902, *GLENBURN*, 1904, *GLENCOE*, 1905, and *GLENBURY*, 1907.

All vessels, in theory, carried a naval officer or at least a non-commissioned army officer, but in the event that was not always possible. The Tug *CRESTED COCK*, Master: Capt T Hills, had left Gravesend for Tilbury on 29th May at 17:15 with no recorded naval officer on board, towing the barges *GLENWAY, SPURGEON* and *LARK*. She anchored at Southend overnight before proceeding to Ramsgate on 30th May and thence to Dover with the barges.

The beaching of sailing barges was necessary to ensure that dumps of water, food and – most vital of all – ammunition, now dangerously low all along the perimeter line, could be supplied to the waiting troops. With little other shelter on the beach troops hid below while they awaited rescue, out of sight of German aeroplanes.

GLENWAY was carrying a consignment of bread, munitions and medical supplies as she crossed the channel towed by the tug

PERSIA along with *LARK* on 31st May. The tow parted on the way across, was re-connected and at 08:00 on 1st June they arrived at East Pier Dunkirk during an air raid. *PERSIA* towed the barges to 1 mile east of the pier head. They sailed ashore independently.

GLENWAY's skipper H Easter beached her at Dunkirk as ordered so that the troops could access the vital supplies. Troops later tried to refloat her without success, until the barge and its desperate soldiers were noticed by Sub. Lieutenant Bruno de Hamel, from an anti-submarine vessel just off shore. Evidently he had some knowledge of sailing, possibly in barges. Be that as it may, showing great courage and resourcefulness he took charge, and with the help of 213 soldiers re-floated her, armed her and commenced a journey that that took 16 dangerous and frightening hours. 20 of those on board died from their injuries during this horrific operation. The last part of her journey was under tow by tug to Dover. De Hamel's heroic action and *GLENWAY* saved 160 - 200 (estimates vary) soldiers of 27 Field Regiment, Royal Artillery.

Alex Smith, coming home on H.A.C. recorded on 2nd June:
   "I could see another barge ahead of us and ENA".
The third barge was probably *GLENWAY*.

There are claims that a ghost has been seen on board. On a moonlit night a man wearing a black heavy overcoat that had turned a greenish colour with age appeared. He was about 50 years old, dark haired and going thin on top, and he had a pallid complexion. He looked for a moment and then disappeared into thin air. Maybe he was one of the poor souls that died at Dunkirk. On 25th January 1974 she was sold to Christopher Bushel from London. In 1978 she was photographed by a John Silfleet whilst moored in the saltings at Strood. Later she was rigged at Ipswich by Steve Barry but then abandoned at Maldon. *GLENWAY* was rescued by G Reeve and sold on to Hugh Poore in 1988, and put on blocks at the Dolphin Yard, Colliers Creek Sittingbourne, Kent.

After the war she led a chequered life with several owners and a lot of money spent on restoration projects. She now lies under private ownership in the mud at Maylandsea, her future uncertain (2009).

Dover harbour [2]

s.b. *SPURGEON*

Sailing barge *SPURGEON* was built in 1883, in 1938 owned by William Theobald of Leigh-on-sea. She was bombed on 29th May as well as damaged by splinters from a near miss whilst under tow for Dunkirk by *CRESTED COCK*. Although history has it that she had to limp home without crossing to France she is listed on the French site of vessels as taking part in Operation Dynamo.

Another truck driver:
> *"I was ordered by an officer to take him back to the front. He had a blind spot I think. He wanted to win the war single handed. We came to a bridge and brigadier told the officer he*

was an idiot. He made him get out and told me to take the truck back to the beach."

As they lay among the dunes, trying to rest, some men dreamed of the terraced suburbs and semi detached houses of south London.

A cook-sergeant came down from La Panne on 31st May:
"I brewed up hard-tack and bully but we had no dixies. I cooked it all on an iron gate over a bonfire".

Safely home [2]

THEY CAME BACK - UNBEATABLE

Daily Express, Friday 31st May 1940:

"Tired, dirty, hungry they came back - unbeatable.

"An army that had been shelled and bombed from three sides, and had to stagger backward into the sea to survive. An army that has been betrayed, but never defeated or dispirited.

"There was a touch of glory about these returning men as I saw them tramping along a pier, still in formation, still with their rifles. For this army still had a grin on their oily, bearded faces.

"They were exhausted. They had not slept or eaten for days. Many tramped off in their stockinged feet. Others were in their shirt sleeves. Many had wounds. Many had torn uniforms, and their tin hats blasted open like a blasted cabbage. They saluted their officers, who stood with ragged macintoshes and battered hats, said 'Thank you sir' Then they left to sleep.

"Their eyes, bloodshot and half closed, still mirrored the spirit and cause of their great fight. That has not gone, nor can it be taken away. How to start telling you of these men? It is the greatest and most glorious sight I have ever seen. I saw them first of all huddled in old tramp steamers, ships of all sorts, even barges in tow.

"The ragged bits of transport had been ploughing backwards and forwards. Germans had chased them halfway over the Channel and in their turn had been chased back.

Young crews volunteered for the job, and the older, local skippers who know the Channel better than the land. Without fear they went into the blast and hell on the other side.

"The men came ashore in heaps, barely able to stand. Yet they pulled themselves into straight lines and walked to the harbour gates."

The story continues:

"Able-Seaman Bradley, of Sunderland: 'We went ashore to search for British troops. We found wounded men lying among the sand dunes. Some were carried into the whalers, while others came wading out up to their necks. Some we had to carry on our (backs) in a hail of bombs.'

"One of the wounded, Private Crighton of Glasgow: 'For days we hid in the dunes, living like rabbits, until the Navy came in and did a grand job of work in getting us away.'

"A young Liverpool private who had force-marched thirty miles a day with a machine-gun bullet in his foot: 'The way those Huns machine-gunned women and children made us mad. I'm going back as soon as this foot's better.'

"A quartermaster-sergeant from Whitley Bay: 'Before we embarked my men marched without sleep for nine days. They bombed us most of the time. The Germans are rotten fighters. When we got a chance with our Bren guns we mowed 'em down. It was slaughter that almost made you sick.'

"When one rescue ship was bombed in a Belgian harbour the crew swam ashore: but when she did not go down they swam back again to take her out of the port. But she turned turtle and they had to swim again. 'I was very thankful' said a seaman 'when after swimming about seven or eight miles I was able to get hold of a table, and another fellow and I sat on it until we were picked up. All of us were almost naked, and we have had no food since yesterday midday, and no sleep for three days. But it's back now to help the Army. It's not only British troops we are bringing off, but French and Belgians too.'

"Some of the men had been bombed out of as many as three ships during the crossing"

In Ramsgate, upon our return from the re-union in 1990 a lady told us about three nights and days in Hastings:

"I was in service, just 18 years old. The daughter of the house was a doctor. She asked for me to help her and milady said she could have me as long as she wanted. We went down to the beach at Ramsgate. The soldiers were coming ashore in rowing boats and little yachts. They were exhausted. Some of them were naked. They were so ashamed because they had to run away but mostly because they were naked in front of us women. The people in the town brought their blankets and sheets and we cuddled them up as best we could and got them off the beach. But I'll never forget those poor men. They were so ashamed. I was on the beach three days and three nights until I was sent home"

Daily Express journalist Hilde Marchant tells of the BEF's return:

"Hospital trains moved through London from the coast all day yesterday (30th May) and far into the night, bringing wounded BEF men back. Those who could sit up waved to people from their carriage windows all along the line".

"People in a row of houses near the harbour, disturbed in the night by the noise, went to see what was happening, then went to help.

"All night and day men and women, and even children, have been standing there with cups of tea, lumps of bread and cigarettes. They paid for them themselves. When stocks ran out they sent schoolboys with barrows round the town appealing for help. These barrows came back piled with food and hundreds of cigarettes.

"Many of the soldiers arrived in only vest and socks. Clothes were gathered up in the town and given to them. One women I talked to said 'It was pitiful when they first came. We had not expected them and we soon ran out of food. They were so hungry that when we gave them just plain dry bread they took it as if it was a whole meal'.

"As the busloads went through the town the men cheered to the crowds and shouted 'Don't worry, we'll get them yet'."

The Daily Express reported that the French were asserting that the fight is going well, and that some Belgians were still fighting, disobeying King Leopold's directive to lay down their arms.

A veteran at Dunkirk in 1990:
"We scrounged a flask of Cointreau off a seaside café owner who had no water to offer. We filled our water bottles with the stuff. When eventually we got on a British ship they swapped some of the Cointreau for cigarettes. We were having a binge, singing and dancing all the way back with the ship steering an erratic course, pretty blotto by the time we got home".

Asked the names of the ships, he couldn't remember:
"We didn't bother about names we were just glad to be alive. Too many of those blokes, mates of ours, have gone west"

British soldiers returning on an un-named barge to Dover [2]

Two chaps told us:

> "A coaster had beached head on, so we, along with over a thousand others clambered aboard. When the tide came in she didn't float so we tried kedging her free. Everyone ran from one side to the other to rock her. Eventually she floated, and we started for home, but a Dornier dropped a torpedo and she was disabled. She drifted towards home. A naval ship found us drifting towards a minefield, so he towed us away and home. I stayed on deck and saw it all. I manned a gun and was credited with three enemy planes shot down".

Even when men got onto a boat they were in extreme danger. Many of those that didn't go down with rescue boats, who were rescued from the water, suffered extensive injuries. The hospitals in Dover quickly filled up with bloodied bodies dying often within hours of arrival. They were tended by hastily recruited nurses of eighteen years old and upwards who had never seen blood or death before. These girls grew up in a hurry.

One chap:
> *"I carried a bloke on to a destroyer and was going back for someone else but an old matelot said 'NO, stay here, we are going soon'. I crashed out and the next thing I remember is waking up in Dover".*

The log of Tug *SUN III* recorded that they left Southend at 12:00 hours on 31st May with 4 Sailing Barges, *HASTE AWAY, ADA MARY, BURTON* and *SHANNON* in tow, taking them down to Ramsgate.

s.b. *HASTE AWAY*
HASTE AWAY was a Thames sailing barge of 46t built in 1886 for James O. Fison, Eastern Union Mills, Ipswich and in 1938 owned by Peters and Co. of Leigh-on-sea, Essex.

The Master of *SUN III*. F. W Russell recorded:
> *"tow and proceeded astern of the DUKE with the Isle of Wight ferry FISHBOURNE which was en route to Dunkirk towed by the tugs PRINCE, PRINCESS and DUKE.*

By the middle of the afternoon they were close to Dunkirk. Air attacks were heavy again, but the master of *DUKE* recording that they were split up by our own fighter aircraft. *HASTE AWAY* returned home from Dunkirk, restored to her owners on 5th June. After the war she was used as a store barge, suffered fire damage in 1957 and finally scrapped in 1972.

TAMZINE, a sailing dinghy built by Brockman & Titcombe, of Margate in Kent, at 14.7ft (4.5m) was the smallest vessel to cross to Dunkirk.

TAMZINE now in Imperial War Museum, London [*]

She was towed back to England by a Belgian Trawler. The skipper may have thought that having a dinghy in tow might come in useful if the trawler was bombed, strafed or hit a mine. Or that the courage of the men who brought her to the rescue operation was so remarkable that she must be saved.

Pandemonium was coined by John Milton as the name of the "high capital of Satan and all his peers" in *Paradise Lost* in 1667.

> *"All the sounds you can think of in a cacophony; whistling, explosions, thuds, cracks, bangs, crashes, screams, roaring and crackling, detonations, flare-ups, blasts, eruptions, upsurges of disharmony. My friend was beside me on the beach. We were there for two days and nights. There was no relief from the noise. He was trying to dig himself into the*

sand with his hands. I dropped off to sleep during the night. When I woke up he was dead. He had died from sheer fright".

The son of this man said:
"My father was an absolute bastard to us children. He didn't tell me about this experience until he was dying. I realised then that it had been his way of hardening us up, trying to prepare us to withstand whatever life might throw at us."

An old soldier:
"I remembered the workhouse cry of almost unimaginable pain as children were dragged away from their mothers. Did it prepare me for the excruciating misery of that beach during those days? I'd have gone back to the workhouse any day".

Another old soldier:
"I came home on a barge that had been carrying coal.
"I was on a train in England when I went to the toilet. I caught sight of this wild, hairy, filthy man looking at me in the toilet mirror and went for my gun. Then I realised it was me!"

Try to imagine the thoughts and feelings of those men. We can only imagine it through our own experience, picture it in our heads. But every man or woman on that beach was an individual. Each had their own priorities, hopes and fears. Some had very little imagining, just did as they were told, kept their heads down 'ploughing a straight furrow' as had been their experience in another life. Some had loved, some had lost love; some had never known it.

"I remember thinking I'd never even had a girl. I wished I'd done that. I made up my mind "If I get through this the first thing I'll do ..."

Major Ogier, an officer from the 4th Hussars:

"We were on the beach two days. On the first night the men went down the beaches into the water until breast high they stretched out to sea like a black pier under the gathering night. After two day a destroyer sent boats to take us off and we finally landed at Ramsgate. Next morning we found ourselves at Bristol with a great crowd of other units; every single man had bacon and eggs for breakfast."

An old soldier spent two nights on the beach:

"I'd drop off maybe thinking about the boys in the pub, or the old lady's flannel nightie. Then as I woke up, for about 30 seconds I would not know where I was. I'd wonder why the bed was so uncomfortable, or why I felt so lousy, and then I'd know and I'd feel sick to my stomach – funny really, considering we were near starving!"

"The worst thing, I think, was thirst. You cannot imagine going without water for two, three days until it happens to you. You get delirious. You see people, smell things, and talk to people who aren't there. I felt lousy most of the time. It wasn't worth getting to sleep; you had nightmares. Some of the men got hold of liquor and fights broke out. People think we were quiet and brave. Some were, but desperate men get ugly, no mistake. But when they died the toughest of them called for their Mother."

A British Soldier wearing a variety of British and French uniforms

THE GLORIOUS 1st JUNE

America woke up to read the New York Times over breakfast on 1st June:

> "So long as the English tongue survives, the word 'Dunkirk' will be spoken with reverence. In that harbour, such a hell on earth as never blazed before, at the end of a lost battle, the rags and blemishes that had hidden the soul of democracy fell away. There, beaten but unconquered, in shining splendour, she faced the enemy, this shining thing in the souls of free men which Hitler cannot command.
> It is the great tradition of democracy.
> It is the future. It is Victory."

Saturday 1st June 1940 is arguably the most memorable in the history of the barges of the east coast waters.

On this day eight barges are recorded lost: *AIDIE, BARBARA JEAN, DUCHESS, ETHEL EVERARD, LARK, ROYALTY, DORIS* and *LADY ROSEBERY*.

s.b. *DUCHESS:*
A Thames sailing barge built in 1904 at East Greenwich and registered in London, *DUCHESS* was originally owned by Clement W. Parker of Bradwell. Clem Parker had followed into the family business as an assistant coal merchant before expanding his business with a fleet of 17 barges operating from Bradwell Quay, including the 55 ton *DUCHESS*. The firm's blue flag containing a white hand on a red heart was one of the best known flags in the River Blackwater. In 1887 he married Ellen Turner from Ipswich, living with his family at Peakes Farm on a high spot overlooking Bradwell Creek and the Quay so that he could keep on eye on his small fleet. In 1940 she was owned by Wakeley Bros.

At low water, about 2.30am on the 1ˢᵗ June, *DUCHESS* beached. In the breaking dawn the soldiers began to board her until 90 men were aboard, the khaki uniforms melting into the red ochre of her sails. Hardly a one had ever set foot on a sailing vessel in their lives, but now their lives depended on English oak managed by skipper H. Wildish and his mate.

As the tide rose *DUCHESS* floated off, but almost immediately the wind died, leaving the sails flapping as the sprit waved to and fro, blocks creaked and ropes slatted idly. We can almost hear the muttered swearing from Skipper Wildish who had no more wish to remain where he was than did the anxious and frightened troops, completely out of an environment they could understand. A destroyer came towards them at speed: the naval commanding officer shouted that he would take the men and ordered Wildish to go back for more. Now the soldiers suffered the terrifying experience of being transferred at sea from a sailing vessel to a naval ship. The drinking water and few rations the barge crew could offer them had restored them somewhat from their exhaustion but a hot drink and food on the destroyer, let alone the feel of a solid deck instead of a rolling one would seem heaven-sent. They would soon see the white cliffs of Dover.

But now *DUCHESS* had nothing left. The galley crew sent over a few supplies, and both ships went their separate ways.

A light breeze enabled *DUCHESS* to get under way. As he trimmed the sails Wilding watched the destroyer move away. So did the Nazi planes circling overhead. The destroyer was bombed without mercy; the men so relieved to be aboard her now faced another danger as they abandoned her and she sunk.

Wilding made for the beach, fully expecting his turn to abandon ship at any moment and hoping he would live to achieve it, but made the shore near to *AIDIE* and *ETHEL EVERARD*, both already abandoned, and *ROYALTY,* still crewed. After hurried consultation both crews took to *DUCHESS*'s rowing boat, setting explosives on the two barges. The Luftwaffe made short work of both of them. This operation was the first time in history that sailing craft had been bombed from the air.

Bedraggled, exhausted disorientated soldiers were tumbling off every train from the south coast into the waiting arms of friends, relatives and sometimes strangers. There were cups of tea a-plenty, rock cakes and doorstep sandwiches, sometimes bacon and eggs waiting for the returning men. Moral must have been at rock-bottom, but such loving kindness restored a man to himself.

A railway station on the Dover to London line, June, 1940 [2]

s.b. *DAWN:*
Built in Maldon, Essex for a local merchant and barge owner, by the jobbing shipwright Walter Cook who took on the shipyard on the River Blackwater at Maldon in 1894, *DAWN* was launched in 1897, as a stackie, displacing 54 tons. The Thames sailing barge had been ordered by James Keeble, a member of a well-known local barge owning family. She took cargoes of mangolds for horse feed to London, returning with manure for the farms.

She was ready for active service in 1939 when she was commandeered by the Government and was loaded with supplies for the BEF fighting in northern France. She was ordered to help evacuate the troops from Dunkirk but whilst in Dover harbour she was in collision with a naval tugboat, started to make water and was obliged to return to her home port. She does nevertheless appear on the register of the Dunkirk Little Ships.

In 1951 she was fitted with a 44hp engine, but when sold to a timber merchants a year or two later was stripped of all her gear and engine. *DAWN* is now based at West Mersea on the River Blackwater Essex and is available for charter. She is a television star, appearing as a stackie carrying a cargo of hay into London in 'River Journeys' with Griff Rhys Jones.

Admiral Wake-Walker came over from Dunkirk by MTB to join the team in the conference room of Operation Dynamo on 1st June. His plan was that there should be one final push, with every vessel sailing for Dunkirk itself to pick up as many as possible. The plan would provide for enough large ships to lift 37,000 men, plus any others picked up by the small boats still going backwards and forwards across the channel.

s.b. *WESTALL:*
s.b *WESTALL* was built in Strood in 1913 and registered at Rochester No: 127259, a 46 ton spritsail she is in Merchant Navy lists of 1938 as owned by London & Rochester Trading Co. There is no other record of her actually crossing to France in 1940. Quite possibly she is listed, with several others, because she was waiting for orders in Dover or Ramsgate, but did not actually go across, although she is named as a wreck in Dunkirk waters. She was owned during the 1990's by John Drew at Hoo Marina.

s.b. *AIDIE:*
The maximum size of barge building was reached in the four Everard barges and R & W Paul's *AIDIE* and *BARBARA JEAN*.

Named after Cyril Paul's daughter, s.b *AIDIE* was a steel hulled barge, built by Aldous & Co. of Brightlingsea in 1924/5 along with *BARBARA JEAN* for R. & W. Paul of Ipswich, a big barge carrying about 280 tons.

Ipswich Port Records show *AIDIE* bound for London with a cargo of maize on 25th May, skipper Harry Potter.

AIDIE beached, with LARK anchored in the distance [II]

Commandeered on the Thames early in the operation she was, like *BARBARA JEAN,* towed to Gravesend to go alongside Tilbury Jetty for degaussing. Loaded with drinking water in cans, military stores and explosives she was towed across by the tug *EMPIRE HENCHMAN.* A steel hulled barge would be the most likely to attract magnetic mines, even after degaussing. Skipper Potter knew that, and must have imagined what would happen if his cargo of ordnance blew up. Nevertheless it was hoped that with supplies the BEF might still make a stand so he whistled under his breath and did his duty.

AIDIE beached between Dunkirk and Le Panne, to discharge her cargo of military stores and then be used as a pontoon. Skipper was ordered to abandon her on 1st June. Skaphandros, a register of wreck data for the diving community, records *AIDIE* in the same way as *BARBARA JEAN* as *"wrecked in 1940, being grounded"*. She was partly blown up and remained in Dunkirk into the 1950's, used as a coal hulk.

Tug *EMPIRE HENCHMAN:* The 'Empire' series were ships in the service of the British Government. Their names were all prefixed with *Empire*. Mostly they were used during the Second World War by the Ministry of War Transport (MoWT), which owned the ships but contracted out their management to various shipping lines. Requisitioned for war service by the Royal Navy, *EMPIRE HENCHMAN* was a tug which was built by Cochrane & Sons Ltd, Selby. She was launched on 31st August 1939 as *KARL* for Goteborgs, Bogserings & Bargnings Akt, Gothenburg. Requisitioned by MoWT and completed in February 1940 as *EMPIRE HENCHMAN,* she operated under the management of United Towing Co Ltd.

s.b. *LARK:*
Built at Greenhithe by F.T. Eberhardt for Thomas Scholey in 1900 and registered in London No: 112735 she is named on the Merchant Navy lists of 1938 as an 81ft. 54 ton spritsail barge remaining in the ownership of T. Scholey & Co. of Greenwich. Her owner is named as A. Fayers by the Thames Tugs Dunkirk website. He may have been her skipper.

Along with *GLENWAY* and *SPURGEON* she had been towed by the tug *CRESTED COCK* to Dover from Gravesend via Tilbury, anchoring at Southend overnight and then on to Ramsgate and Dover.

Gravesend 1935[10]

Southend Pier had been built of wood when it was opened in 1830, and 600 feet long. By 1833 it had been extended to three times its length and by 1848 was the longest pier in Europe at 7,000 feet. During World War II the Pier was taken over by the Royal Navy and was renamed (along with the surrounding area) HMS *WESTCLIFF*.

Southend Pier 1935[10]

The pier was closed to the public on 9th September 1939. Its purpose in the war was twofold. Firstly it served as a mustering point for convoys. Over the course of the war 3,367 convoys, comprising 84,297 vessels departed from HMS *WESTCLIFF*.

Secondly, it was Naval Control for the Thames Estuary. Notable in its career was the accidental sinking of the Liberty ship the The wreck of SS *RICHARD MONTGOMERY*, still containing several thousand tons of explosives, is visible from the North Kent coast and Southend beach at low tide, and continues to pose a threat to navigation and the surrounding area to this day.

LARK took on board the cargo of *s.b. CENTAUR,* which had been damaged, delivered the water to the waiting troops and was beached at Dunkirk on 1st June, as ordered. She was later brought home.

a.b. *SHERFIELD:*

This barge sailed from Sheerness on 1st June. Having rescued some 70 troops she came under attack by German fighters on the return trip. Shutting off her engines, the crew and the men on board 'lay doggo', allowing the barge to drift so that she appeared abandoned. It is hard to imagine the discipline required to lie still, whether above or below decks, as they were under fire from enemy aircraft. The ruse worked, however, and the enemy few off in search of more rewarding prey. She is not registered on MNL.

s.b. *ADA MARY:*

Thames sailing barge *ADA MARY,* 44tons, built in 1887 for Smeed Dean & Co. of Sittingbourne in Kent, was owned by the Leigh Building Co. In 1938 she was owned by William Theobald of Leigh-on-sea.

Log of *SUN III* on 1st June:
> "*Abreast of the South Falls the stern most barge HASTE AWAY again broke adrift and was taken in tow by the tug DUKE which was in company.*
> "*At 12:00 the aftermost barge ADA MARY broke adrift and was taken in tow by the tug DUKE. The tow broke but was reconnected. The FISHBOURNE was now out of sight.*"

Tug *DUKE* confirms:

> "Off Broadstairs the HASTE AWAY and ADA MARY broke adrift but were picked up. (We) arrived Ramsgate at 17:15. On 1st June (we) left Ramsgate at 09.15 with 4 barges in tow".

ADA MARY returned home and was later used as Sea Cadet HQ at Newhaven until 1990.

FISHBOURNE was a Car Ferry, owned by the Southern Railway. Built by Wm. Denny, Dumbarton, in 1927 she was thought to have been scrapped in 1962.

s.b. *BURTON:*

The sailing barge *BURTON,* 44 tons, was built by Smeed Dean of Murston, Kent, in 1880 and registered at Rochester at 48 tons. Length 75ft 0ins, beam 17ft depth 5ft and her official number 81867 (PLA number was 14046). She was rebuilt at Murston in 1914 and sold to Associated Portland Cement Manufacturers by 1934. She was sold to Leigh Building Company for £50 in May 1935 (equivalent to £2,249 in 2002) and was owned by William Theobald of Leigh on Sea, Essex, in 1938. In 1940 her owners were the Leigh Building Company.

BURTON'S skipper recorded:

> "1st June. Later we met up with the Isle of Wight ferry FISHBOURNE towed by the tugs PRINCE, PRINCESS and DUKE. As our tug, SUN III was having a lot of trouble with our four barges breaking adrift; the DUKE was detached from FISHBOURNE to pick up the barges HASTE AWAY and ADA MARY leaving SUN III to manage BURTON and SHANNON. After being attacked by enemy aircraft FISHBOURNE was ordered back to Ramsgate." ('Dunkirk Relived' by Arthur Joscelyne published by SSBR Topsail magazine No. 23, 1987.)

There is no more information on the part she played during the operation. She likely carried water, biscuits and/or ammunition. After the war *BURTON* was used as a store barge and finally burnt in 1957.

BURTON in Small Gains Creek taken in 1957 - Ray Rush Collection [7]

s.b *SHANNON:*
SHANNON, was built in 1898 at Milton-next-Sittingbourne, registered in London No: 109920, a Spritsail barge of 57 tons by Alfred White for Hilton Anderson Brooks and Co. of Halling. In 1907 she was owned by The Associated Portland Cement Manufacturers of Fenchurch Street, London. Her dimensions were 86.7 ft. x 20.6ft x by 6.2 ft. The 1938 MNL gives her owner as Arthur J. Peters of Southend.

The records pertaining to tug *SUN III* state that *SHANNON* was a Thames sailing barge, owned by W. McCormack, although he may have been her master during the crossing. On 31st May the tug *SUN III*, her master F W Russell, left Southend for Ramsgate with 4 sailing barges, *HASTE AWAY*, *ADA MARY*, *BURTON* and *SHANNON* in tow.

At 12:30 on 1st June as *SUN III* approached the Outer Ruytingen Buoy, with now only *BURTON* and *SHANNON* in tow they were again under enemy air attack, which this time was dispersed by our own fighter planes. The tug embarked 20 solders from a lifeboat. At 17:00 they were directed by a plane to 2 boats full of soldiers near the Whistle Buoy on Le Dyke off Gravelines, one load taken by *SUN III*. The other boat load was taken by *DUKE*.

At 21:30 *SUN III* decided to return to Ramsgate. *SHANNON* was still under tow, as she broke adrift off Broadstairs on the way home but was picked up, although damaged. The account does not make clear what part she may have played in either servicing or rescuing troops at Dunkirk during the evident confusion.

On June 2/3rd *SUN III* returned to Ramsgate with 148 stained and dripping wet khaki-clad troops on board who came ashore in launches on 3rd June.

Montgomery faced serious trouble from his military superiors and the clergy for his frank attitude regarding the sexual health of his soldiers, but was defended from dismissal by his superior Alan Brooke, commander of II Corps. Monty's 3rd Infantry Division was deployed to Belgium as part of the BEF Realizing that the British and the French had little intention to invade Germany, he predicted a defeat should Germany decide to invade France, and trained his troops for tactical retreat, which paid off when the men of the 3rd Infantry Division effectively fell back toward the French coast with great professionalism, entering the Dunkirk perimeter in a famous night-time march which placed his forces on the left flank which had been left exposed by the Belgian surrender. The 3rd Division returned to Britain intact with minimal casualties. During Operation Dynamo he assumed command of the II Corps as Alan Brooke, the previous commanding officer, became the acting commander of the BEF now re-assembling in England in readiness to defend against the expected German invasion. Monty was noticed to be imperturbable in adversity. When the position of his men looked desperate he was still cocky and full of confidence that he could carry out the orders given to him and he had the gift of being able to convey this certainty to his men. II Corps maintained a rearguard action until the last moment, and Monty and his men were among the last to be evacuated on 1st. June.

ONE SMALL HOPE

At 10 am on 2nd June Ramsey signalled the whole command:
"The final evacuation is staged for tonight, and the Nation looks to the Navy to see this through. I want every ship to report as soon as possible whether she is fit and ready to meet the call which has been made on our courage and endurance."

Back came the replies:
"Ready and anxious to carry out your order"…. "Fit and ready"….
Despite the brave response most hearts sank. The sailors had thought that yesterday was 'one last effort'. But:
"We were going and that was all there was to it".

The crews of the *BEN-MY-CHREE, MALINE* and *TYNWALD*, passenger channel steamers from Folkstone gesticulated and shouted, crowding the rails to threaten to leave their ships. They were virtually unarmed and, obviously not built as a fighting force but with wide decks, presented the biggest targets at Dunkirk. The *MALINE*, with no authority at all, slipped her berth and sailed for Southampton.

a.b. *MARIE MAY:*

Registered at Rochester on the Medway, No: 127270 as 83 tons, *MARIE MAY* was built of wood at Maidstone by Hutson in 1920. *MARIE MAY* was sold to the London and Rochester Trading Co. (LRTC) described as a barge at 76 tons she was the last barge to be built at that yard and possibly the largest. In 1929 Dungeness Lifeboat Coxswain Douglas Oiller received a Bronze Medal for a service to the barge *MARIE MAY*. She is mentioned as an auxiliary barge fitted with a 66hp Kelvin engine in 1931 that is, having both sail and motor energy. There is little or no information about her participation in Operation Dynamo.

She is said to be the first barge to trade in Sandwich after the war, following her release from war time duties in 1949. She went up to the Clyde during the Second World War acting as lighter and transporting military stores and mail boats to the Cunarders, *QUEEN MARY* and *QUEEN ELIZABETH* which were working as transatlantic troop ships; and, back south, she traded around the Thames and Medway, up to Essex ports, and also to Ipswich.

She retired from trade as a motor barge in the 1960's. She was owned by G. Lynch in the 1990's and used as a house-barge, at West Cowes, re-rigged and was apparently moored somewhere around the Isle of Wight; Wootton Creek and West Cowes are given. She is understood to have been wrecked at the former Belsize boat yard in Southampton.

s.b. *ENA:*
ENA of Ipswich, Registration number on MNL 122974, (Ipswich Register Ref: 01/1907), length 88.9ft, displacement 79 tons was built in 1905/6 at Harwich by W.B. McLearon jnr. for R. & W. Paul Ltd. of Ipswich, in 1963 (Paul's Foods Ltd., in 1973 Pauls & Sanders, Pauls and Whites Ltd 1974). She is a wooden square stern two mast spritsail barge, originally mulie rigged and later converted to spritsail (staysail).

Peter Shaw, an ex-employee of Paul's:
"The Paul's fleet had traditionally been named for the women in the Paul family. ENA would often sail down to London to collect the grain off Canadian ships, carrying back 265 ton of grain. She was used as a stacki, or mulie. They laid boards out the sides, and loaded her half way up the mast with straw, all the way round and hanging out the side, a haystack on the move. She would take the straw up to London, where we had horses, and often bring the muck back to put on the land that Paul's owned. If they didn't bring muck back they would bring grain."

Ipswich Port records show *ENA*, a mulie barge, Skipper Alfred Page, left for London 25th May, with mate Arthur 'Scatty' Catchpole.

Asked whether he would volunteer for the crossing to Dunkirk, 'Titch' Page immediately agreed. For one thing he didn't want to leave his barge, and for another he would have been bitterly disappointed not to be included in this dangerous assignment.

In Dover she was loaded with petrol in two gallon cans. She was in effect a floating bomb. Enduring constant air attacks, and with the sea around them strewn with mines, knowing that one hit would blow her and everyone on her to smithereens, Titch Page was at the helm during the outward journey across the English Channel. Trying to avoid or divert certain death from minefields or aerial attack, *ENA* was late to arrive.

Mr. Page was ordered to beach her close to the smaller sand barge *H.A.C.* As the Germans closed in, the crews of both barges were ordered to abandon their ships and get back England; *ENA* still loaded with cans full of petrol.

The crews reluctantly accepted a lift back home by the minesweeper, assured that this was their last chance of escape. Trying to imagine the mind blowing dangers and uncertainty they had so far endured, it is difficult to imagine them being 'reluctant' to get the heck out of it, but they evidently were made of stern stuff and they took their time.

On the night of 1st June a group of men from the 19th Field Regiment Royal Artillery, and the 1st Battalion the Duke of Wellington's Regiment, the last survivors of the perimeter defence were making their way to the beach without much hope of rescue, saw the two barges, the only serviceable seagoing vessels in a scenario nightmare of death and chaos. The sight of two sailormen lying at anchor, even without crews, meant that all hope was not lost.

All hope was not lost [8]

The following is a first hand account given in 1992 by Eric Stuart of the 1st Lancs Regiment:

"We had assembled finally to the beaches awaiting being picked up in anything that was sailing and the last boat had finally left as it was too dangerous to assemble by day, it had to take place by night as this particular part of the beach was under shell fire. However when dawn broke there were groups of people lying where shells had landed but not much could be done therefore what men were present were detailed as stretcher bearers taking wounded and dead up to the more sheltered parts of the beach front into houses and so forth. This went on for most of the time until the beaches were cleared (of men) and there were no more signs of any movement of any description.

"There was no point anywhere of assembling on the beach if there was no boat in sight except for one vessel anchored out, that one small hope. It looked lifeless but as it was there most of the day and no movement towards evening I decided to swim out to investigate, not sure if it was a local fishing vessel.

"I eventually reached it and clambered aboard only to find it empty there were signs of a half eaten meal no crew. I jumped overboard and swam back and rounded up what few people I could see and explained the situation as it was now everyman for himself and the only chance available.

"I managed to convince a few of what the chances were and so they made it with me and with their help I had to make out how the sails were hoisted. The jib was easy but the mainsail took a bit of puzzling over, but we weren't quite ready for that until everything was right to raise the anchor.

"Meanwhile others had gone back to shore to pick up any more survivors willing to take a chance and they managed to pick up a few more and in all around thirty or forty persons were aboard."

Colonel McKay with men of the 19th Field Regiment, Royal Artillery boarded the ENA. The colonel (later awarded the OBE and the Military Cross) ordered the first task of the Gunners should be the unloading of the dangerous cargo.

Captain Atley of the East Yorks Regiment:

"I was at the Mole at Dunkirk and together with one of my men, made a raft out of bits and pieces of equipment on the beach. We rowed out to the ENA using shovels. We helped 36 other men on board including three wounded; unloaded the petrol cans and she floated off. By 08:00 on the 2nd June we were under sail."

Eric Stuart continues:

"Dawn was breaking and we decided it was time to lift the anchor. The tide had turned and we were heading out to sea. We eventually had the sails hauled up but unfortunately there was only a breath of wind but what there was took us further away from the coast of Dunkirk and towards Britain, but it seemed an awfully slow process.

"For a start the boat seemed sluggish but at least we had the mainsail up and left the topsail furled in case of a sudden storm and danger of capsizing as my previous sailing experience was with sailing dinghies. I had previously sailed with the Royal Navy but there was no experience of sailing a boat of this class but fortunately (everything) seemed to work.

"All the men were made to stay below in the hold out of sight which later proved fortunate. Although the drone of aircraft overhead was so high up one couldn't make out what they were until very suddenly out of the sun a plane opened fire on us and gave us a burst of machine gun fire. I lay flat behind the wheel and felt I was hit in the back but (it) appeared to be only a piece of wood splinter as the bullets ripped along the decks. After that all was quiet as the plane headed back towards Dunkirk.

"We had on one occasion seen a lifeboat full of dead men laying on the bottom of the boat but we couldn't do anything as we needed all our facilities to get towards the Straights of Dover, and sure enough we could see the outline of Dover Castle. It could have been a mirage but at least there was land ahead. If it wasn't for the fact that it was war it would have been a lovely summer outing but the men were huddled below out of sight fortunately as we could be visited again by any marauding enemy aircraft, and so we drew gratefully nearer the English coast still a long way off.

"The last sight of Dunkirk we would see were puffs of smoke on the beaches where we left, like shell bursts, and small tanks darting about and I am certain they would have rounded up prisoners either able or wounded. I am sure no other boat of any description could have come within landing distance.

Captain Atley:
"By midnight we took a back-bearing on Dunkirk and found we had gone too far South-West. My only sailing experience had been on the Broads and I had forgotten to put the leeboards down. So we altered course to North-Northwest and finally sighted the North Goodwin buoy, then had to tack again towards the South Goodwin lightship."

Eric Stuart goes on:
"We got nearer and nearer the coast and were watching for a place to land when we were apprehended by a trawler that threw a tow line while a member of their crew jumped and made the tow line fast then went back to the trawler. He said if we had continued our course we would have gone through a minefield and mined beaches so the danger wasn't exactly over even then, and to prove it after about fifteen minutes the trawler had almost gone out of sight when we found the tow line had broken however they connected it up again and left a man aboard with us but it wasn't long after when the tow line snapped again. I feel sure it was a heavy boat to tow or was sluggish due to barnacles, I don't know, but we eventually landed at Ramsgate.

"It was just getting dusk and there on shore were women and girls walking along as if there never was a war God bless them. But of the crossing I think we were fortunate to have survived. We left Dunkirk just before dawn and landed at Ramsgate about 10 o'clock in the evening.

"The last thing I did on the harbour wall was to look for the name of the vessel which I couldn't see on the front but on the stern was unmistakeably the name 'ENA' in plain varnished latter with no port of registry visible. Never thinking I would see it again, but the name never left my mind and on the day when I saw the display in the dock (Maritime Ipswich 1990) it

brought tears to my eyes. Since then I went back to France through Normandy right up to the capitulation of Germany just outside Hamburg where it was to be declared an open city with no shot fired.
"Signed Eric Stuart, 348, Wellington Court, Ipswich IP1 2NS. My present age in June 1992 is 82."

It should be remembered that a Thames barge requires a very particular kind of seamanship, learned by experience, and quite unlike any other kind of sailing. To any other sailor the difficult handling would normally be the stuff of nightmares, but these were desperate times. The soldiers sailed them back in a straight line, using a child's atlas and three pocket compasses, covering the most hazardous course that is ever likely to be sailed. Mines were everywhere, Stuka dive bombing was relentless and German artillery mercilessly pounded the beaches and shoreline with shrapnel.

Tug *KENIA*'s owners were William Watkins Ltd, her Master was W. Hoiles and his crew worked to exhaustion during the evacuation. Her log records that on 29th May at 18:20 a Fleet Air Army plane was sighted floating 2 miles from the South Goodwin Light Vessel. *KENIA* took her in tow, but at 19:05 a bomb dropped from the planes rack and exploded astern. At 20:45 near No 3 Ramsgate Buoy the planes stern parted from the body.

KENIA returned to harbour and continued back and forth across the channel with very little rest during the ensuing days. She picked up the skoot *RIAN* loaded with wounded soldiers on 30th May, and piloted her towards Ramsgate Harbour, also towing the broken down skoot *RUJA*.

She left Ramsgate again that day and from the Downs towed the abandoned M/Y *INSPIRATION II* to Ramsgate Channel, where she was handed over to the tug *DORIA* who took her in to Ramsgate. On 31st May 1940 she sighted 2 motor launches 2 miles from the South Goodwin Light Vessel, they were the *R.59* and the *R.36* and had been abandoned.

ENA on the River Colne September 1980. Photo Caroline Rudge *

Harold Russell, mate, KENIA WW2. Photo Harold Russell Jnr. who manned this Lewis gun in action, vulnerable from incoming enemy fire and from the hawser if she was towing [6]

She towed them in to Ramsgate before resuming patrol. On 2nd June she sighted the Swedish S.S. *EMMA* sinking but could give no assistance but buoyed the position. At 20:00 the same day her log recorded:

> *"Sighted the S/B ENA near the South Goodwin Light Vessel with BEF on board who have sailed her from Dunkirk without any sailors to assist."*

ENA was taken in tow by *KENIA* towards Ramsgate, where she disembarked her soldiers. Since the harbour was full, the empty barge was then towed clear of the harbour and left anchored off Deal on the Sandwich Flats with no-one on board; providentially the fine weather held.

The shipping manager of R & W Paul, who had presumed the *ENA* was lost on the beaches of Dunkirk, was amazed when he received a message from the authorities at Deal. She was at anchor in the roads with no-one aboard, they said, and what was he going to do about it?

Alfred Page, her skipper, by then back in Ipswich, was sent to recover her. He found the *ENA* seaworthy, almost unscathed but stripped of all her gear, abandoned on Sandwich Flats. Alfred, in common with other Suffolk sailormen, had a low opinion of Kentish counterparts, particularly those from Deal.

> *"They had taken the sweeps, mooring lines, fenders and even my false teeth which I had left behind in a glass of water by my bunk!"* he said, *"you can't trust these men of Kent!"*

BS.C.4.   11th June, 1940.

H.L. Collard, Esq.,
    Chief of Executive,
        Port of London, Lighterage Emergency Executive,
        P.L.A. Building,
            Trinity Square,
                London, E.C.3.

Dear Sir,

We are in receipt of your letter of the 6th instant asking us for particulars of services rendered by our craft in connection with the evacuation of troops from France. Five of our barges went over to Dunkirk :-

"AIDIE"   Abandoned on the beach between La Panne and Dunkirk.
"BARBARA JEAN" Abandoned at Dunkirk.
"DORIS"   Blown up at Dunkirk
"ENA"   Abandoned at Dunkirk but since arrived off Deal damaged and ordered to Ipswich for repairs.
"TOLLESBURY"   Brought about 200 soldiers over to Gravesend, damaged and ordered to Ipswich.

The barge "AIDIE" took stores over and went on to the beach between La Panne and Dunkirk. The crew was ordered to abandon ship and go on to a Destroyer. The Officer in charge said that the barge was to be abandoned and blown up.

The "BARBARA JEAN" also took stores over and the crew to come out of her and it is understood that she was blown up a...

The "DORIS" in company with two other barges was towed over to Dunkirk. The tug which took them was blown up just after casting off the barges and the DORIS was sunk.

The barge "ENA" went over to Dunkirk and the crew were taken out of her and brought home and the barge has since arrived off Deal. We think that she must have brought some soldiers over.

The barge "TOLLESBURY" went to Dunkirk. The crew ran the barge on to the beach and took on board about 200 soldiers. They then pushed off with setting booms and set sail but could make

P.T.O.

no headway against wind and tide and had to anchor. A Destroyer came alongside to take the men off but there was a terrible Air Raid and the Destroyer had to go away.

Two other Destroyers came along to screen the craft but both were sunk. Bombs dropped all round the barge but it was not hit. Eventually a tug came and got a wire rope aboard but it started too fast and pulled the windlass out. She got another wire aboard and eventually arrived safely in England.

The Captain says the crew, a Mate of 40 and Cook of 19, were marvellous, doing everything in their power to handle the barge and assist soldiers, who were waist deep in the water, aboard.

We are glad to say that the crews of all our barges returned safely.

        Yours truly,
    For R. & W. PAUL, LTD.

The Port of London, Lighterage Emergency Executive

TEL: MANsion House 9111-2.
W. TAYLOR,
SECRETARY.

HPR/EDJ.

P.L.A. BUILDING,
TRINITY SQUARE,
LONDON. E.C.3.

15th June, 1940.

Messrs. R. & W. Paul Ltd.,
   Ipswich,
      Suffolk.

Dear Sirs,

    We have for acknowledgement your letter of the 11th instant wherein you kindly gave us particulars of the services rendered by your five Sailing Barges during the Dunkirk Evacuation.

    This is most interesting to us, and for your information the particulars you have given us will be reported to the Flag Officer-in-Charge, London.

                  Yours faithfully,

                  W. Kolotton

             Assistant to Chief of Executive.

Copies of letters between Pauls & the PLA after Dunkirk.(Courtesy Mr.J.Bear).   9

Ipswich Port records show her returning to Ipswich 10th June from Pegwell Bay. Both she and *TOLLESBURY*, with their usual skippers went straight to the shipyard for maintenance, *ENA* sailing light for London on 22nd July and *TOLLESBURY* lightering from Butterman's Bay on the River Orwell from 2nd to 7th July, sailing to London on 12th August.

In the late 1940's *ENA* was fitted with a Ruston & Hornsby 4cyl 80hp diesel engine, in an engine room of 14.0', and traded to 1973 when Pauls & Whites Ltd laid up their fleet of ex sailing barges.

The vessels, comprising of *ENA, THALATTA, JOCK, ORINOCO* and *LADY DAPHNE* lay for sometime at the lock end of the Ipswich Wet Dock while their fate was decided. It was at this time that the Social Section of Pauls' were looking for a club house/meeting place and the idea was spawned that a barge, especially a rigged barge would be the ideal vehicle for this purpose. George Paul agreed to give them the use of *ENA* and a volunteer band of workers, with help and advice from Harold Smy and Charlie Webb, restored this historic vessel, cleaning her, fitting a new transom, making her seaworthy and re-rigging her.

The new transom [8]   *Charlie Webb re-rigging ENA* [8]

ENA continued under Pauls & Whites ownership until the mid 1990's used for company events and social events, competing in sailing barge races on the Thames, the Medway, Blackwater and Orwell keeping the great tradition of the spritsail barges alive.

ENA took part in the 35th anniversary celebrations of Operation Dynamo in 1975, and the 50th anniversary crossing in 1990.

ENA crossing to Dunkirk, 1990 *

The annual repair & maintenance survey in the winter of 1995/96 identified that extensive – and expensive – repair work was required and the then owners of Pauls & Whites, Elementis, decided to dispose of her. *ENA* was sold to Robert Deards in 2001 then to Luke Deards in 2002 and was the subject of a Channel 4 Salvage Squad programme in 2002. Sadly she now lies in a sorry state in a Kent creek, however she has been purchased by two of Charlie Webb's grandsons, Peter and John Webb, and is to be restored once more. The Webb family possess the flag carrying *ENA*'s name brought home from Dunkirk.

ENA, 2010 *

s.b. H.A.C. (INVICTA):
This smallish barge of 55 tons is referred to as a sand barge by the records of tug *SUN XII*. She was built in Sittingbourne in 1896 for William Prescott of Dover, and registered as 'Spritsail barge *INVICTA*' in that town, No: 105551. She was sold to Erith and Dartford by 1934 and to H. Cunis by 1938. Mr. Cunis owned a barge yard as well as other barges, and changed *INVICTA'S* name to *H.A.C.* to reflect his name, Horace Albert Cunis. She was not registered on MNL as *H.A.C.* but in 1938 *INVICTA* is registered as owned by Mr. Cunis. After the war *H.A.C.* was used as a dredging hopper at Ramsgate.

Still a sailing barge in 1940, her skipper was R. Scott. On 29th May *SUN XII* log recorded that she left Tilbury at 12:00 for Ramsgate and on to Dover towing the a.b. *THYRA* and s.b's *ROYALTY*, *H.A.C.* and *BEATRICE MAUD*. She towed the four barges towards Dunkirk, *H.A.C.* loaded with food and water. *H.A.C.* was beached as ordered and skipper R. Scott was taken off with his crew by the auxiliary barge *THYRA*.

Alex Smith:
> "With 30 men of the Duke of Wellington's Regiment commanded by Captain David Strangeways our Adjutant, I arrived on La Panne beach. We could not believe our luck when we saw two barges in seaworthy condition anchored and almost afloat. We took possession of the barge H.A.C. while Colonel McKay with his men of the 19th Field Regiment, Royal Artillery boarded the ENA which was beached not far away."

While the East Yorks Regiment were engaged in re-floating *ENA*, Colonel L.C.Griffith-Williams salvaged s.b *H.A.C.*, ordered the food and water taken off, re-loading it with artillerymen and she was refloated. She then set of for Britain.

A mysterious story is recalled in 'The Miracle of Dunkirk' by Walter Lord:
> "36 men of the 1st Duke of wellington's regiment taking over a barge called 'IRON DUKE'."

It can only be assumed that the men re-named a barge after their own regiment, that of the 'Iron Duke', whilst they were on board. Alex Smith:
> "The two ships got involved in one of the most remarkable barge races of all time. We were under constant enemy bombardment and machine-gun fire as we crossed the Channel."

The temporary skipper knew nothing about navigation but found a child's atlas aboard. Three men had rudimentary compasses. That would be enough. When a patrol boat later intercepted them they were heading for Germany.

On a glorious June day the men stripped off their dripping and soiled battledress lounged about in the sunshine drinking the water that they had reserved for themselves out of Skipper Scott's battered saucepan. It is reported that the colonel, mindful of his position in life:

> *"maintained his status with a strip of threadbare carpet, worn sarong style, that had been discovered on the cabin floor".*

In proper military style two watches were appointed, with qualified signallers. The water around them was teeming with wreckage. Alex Smith:

> *"We spotted a motor boat from whom we could ask directions. By the time we identified it as an enemy E-boat and prepared to turn and run, we realised that the crew lay dead on deck. I could see another barge ahead of us and ENA."*

The third barge was probably *GLENWAY*.

Lucky to survive the appalling, constant air attacks that went on that day, but with the Red Ensign at the mizzen peak and with a fine beam wind they sighted the white cliffs of Dover at about 4pm, as heartfelt cheers went up. She was eventually towed back to Dover '*by an obliging minesweeper*' with 100 troops on board.

Later the same day *ST. ABBS* picked up some of the troops who had been rescued by HMS *SKIPJACK*, a Halcyon class minesweeper full of rescued troops, which had been bombed, when a further bombing attack was made on the survivors in the water. Able Seaman William Cornford, 41, from Cosham, was among the 20 crew members killed. He is remembered on the Portsmouth Naval Memorial. Nearly all the troops were below decks and few survived. A tug picked up a few of the men struggling in the oily, fire filled water, before she was hit by bombs and sank immediately. Even the men rescued were horribly burnt.

"OPERATION COMPLETED, RETURNING TO DOVER"

"I heard a group of men singing hymns. 'Eternal Father Strong to Save' I think it was. We was all brought up to respect the church and it was a comfort, that's the truth".

Five times before the church service ended the congregation of men, now mainly the rearguard was scattered by low-flying aircraft.

"The beach was littered with all sorts of stuff. There were civilians there as well as us, a few women and children hoping to be taken off. Of course they had their belongings, suitcases broken open, a bit of china, something lacy, pretty things. There were horses as well, I suppose pulling carts or gun carriages I don't know. It was horrible hearing them shot – bang – wait a minute – bang – another one down. In the hot weather they soon were covered in flies. I can't see a big fat bluebottle now without a shiver. The town was pretty deserted so of course the dogs had no food and they looked for people to help them."

At least two women were taken off. Elaine Madden aged 17 was the daughter of a British gardener employed by the War Graves Commission at Poperinghe who had stayed behind to tend the graves when her father had joined the British Army. She and her mother's sister, Simone Duponselle, were smuggled on board a steamer. They were spotted by an alert fellow on the look out for fifth-columnists, but after explaing to the captain they were allowed to stay aboard.

A signal received from Dunkirk read:
"C in C says it is essential that rearguard BEF embarks from the beaches east of Mole on account of French congestion. Considerable number of British troops still on Mole. Military

are expecting further arrivals there. Rearguard expects to arrive at 2.30am."

Many of the stretcher wounded on the beach up to this moment had of necessity to be left behind. A stretcher took up as much room as three fit men. The flow home of wounded virtually ceased this morning.

> "The orders were passed round for the wounded to be left behind for the Germans to take care of. That was a laugh if it wasn't so tragic. I never saw my mate again".

Some of these men had never squashed a fly. Now they had killed other men, other soldiers. They were not there by choice like to today's armed forces, they were conscripts. A conscientious objector was detested as a coward.

Scott Bradly told us:
> "All we know about my grandad's experience at Dunkirk was that he was wounded and that he did no more war service. He never would talk about it. Was he perhaps ashamed that he came back when others didn't, or that he didn't continue the fight, or was it that what he saw caused what we now call 'post traumatic stress'? I am a serviceman myself now and I understand it better. I have mates who completely block it out. One wife was amazed, after seven years of marriage, to hear her husband had been in Bosnia. She just couldn't believe it. But it came out later when he suddenly became violent."

The names of the medical personnel to stay with them were placed in a hat and three brave men stayed behind. A communication was sent to the German Command stating that the wounded situation was acute and that hospital ships would enter Dunkirk during the day with the Geneva Convention honourably observed. The Southern Railway steamer *WORTHING*, now a hospital carrier, left the Downs at 12.55 pm at 20 knots. At 2.32pm, in flagrant contempt of the appeal, she was attacked by twelve enemy aircraft, despite the fact that she was carrying all the marks and signs of a hospital ship. The Geneva Convention had been flouted continuously throughout the evacuation, as it had on countless occasions previously.

A similar disastrous fate met the hospital ship *PARIS*. Built in 1913 for the London, Brighton and South Coast Railway she was transferred to the Southern Railway in 1923, after use as a mine layer during the First World War. She worked out of Brighton between the wars, taking day trippers out from the Palace Pier. She was converted to a hospital ship in 1940 and began transporting the wounded from Dunkirk on 25th May. The crew always went ashore to search for wounded, bringing them aboard, bound for home. On one occasion a train carrying wounded had been abandoned by its French train driver half a mile from the station. A crew member, Stephen Lewis, walked down the line and drove the train and all the wounded to the station from where the wounded were taken aboard the *PARIS*.

Hospital ship PARIS *

Captain Donald Johnson who served in the Royal Army Medical Corps gave the following to the Forces war Records website:
"In May 1940 I was serving in the Hospital Carrier PARIS at Dunkirk to remove the sick and wounded. At that time the most unpleasant place this side of hell was the foreshore and

the sea that lay off the little stretch of coast between La Panne and Dunkirk for the area, thick with weary soldiers and ships of all sizes, was under constant artillery and air attack whilst, later on, German heavy machine guns added their contribution to the general beastliness as their bullets spattered the water with an effect like showers of pebbles from the shore.

"Although the Carrier was clearly marked as a hospital ship it received the same treatment as other vessels and conditions on the Carrier were far from pleasant but there was a job to be done and the crew, doctors and nursing staff went on with it quietly, doing their best to turn deaf ears to the roar of battle going on around them. Their only defence lay in our 'tin hats' and the only sign of panic came from one or two shell-shocked patients who, having come so far, found these last hours of waiting more than they could bear. Among the crew and staff of the Carrier there was nothing but calm efficiency, as more and more wounded men were brought on board and given such treatment as was possible.
I made at least five trips in the ships boats to the open beaches to collect casualties for which I, along with many others later received the George Cross."

It is also of interest that No 15 Field Ambulance based at Lingfield, Surrey took part in the film 'DUNKIRK' and played the part of No 5 and No 6 Field Ambulances which had joined together to help anyone that they could. Most of them were captured with their patients.

On the 2nd June, on her sixth trip into Dunkirk, during the last efforts to get the wounded home the defenceless hospital ship was unmercifully bombed by German Stukers. She suffered extensive bombing by more than fifteen enemy 'planes while approaching France despite being clearly marked as a hospital ship.

As she drifted out of control, with her engine room badly damaged the Dynamo room sent tugs to her aid, including *SUN XV*. The tug *SUN IV* searched for the wounded ship, locating her on 3rd June. Her log records:
> *"01:00 Located PARIS, she was abandoned. Air Attack decided with SUN XV that PARIS being heavily down by the stern and would require an escort, Proceeded homeward with SUN XV towing."*

PARIS sank 10 miles from the shore. The crew had time to lower her lifeboats and everyone was evacuated to eventual safety save a cabin boy, aged 17. One lifeboat was again bombed and the survivors of this barbaric attack were picked up by another tug boat returning to England.

An old soldier remembered her:
> *"I drove most of the way to the beach in one vehicle or another until about two miles out of Dunkirk, then walked the rest. I found Hospital Ship PARIS in one of the dock basins, and asked to be allowed on board. They said 'Yes, if there is a place at the last minute and if you disable your rifle', which I did. I didn't get a place though.*
>
> *"PARIS was bombed on her next attempt although she displayed the Red Cross. I wandered about for two days and found the Mole. Men were guarding it – had been doing so for two days without a break. I got on a British warship, and from then I have total amnesia. I was stopped several times in London for being improperly dressed."*

On the evening of 2nd June, with the German forces closing in, Ramsay despatched a large force of ships, including 13 passenger ships, 14 minesweepers and 11 destroyers.

At 11:30 pm Captain Tennant sent the historic signal from Dunkirk: *"BEF evacuated."*
Conversation with another old soldier:

"I have tried to forget the unpleasant experiences No writing can convey the smells of bodies of animals as well as humans, friends, the sense of fear, sometimes even terror, the fatigue, weight of equipment, pain of blisters on feet, feeling unwashed and being lousy at times, the feel of thick khaki flannel shirts against a sensitive skin on a hot sticky day, the squeal of the tracks of German Tiger tanks, the memories of which caused me to twitch for many years until quite recently. Fortunately, time seems to veil the senses".

The British rearguard left that night along with 60,000 French soldiers. Around 3,000 - 4,000 of the BEF remained on shore. The number of French was uncertain, but estimated to be 25,000 and rising.

s.b. *BASILDON:*
A sailing Barge owned by Leigh Building Co. she is not on MNL list. She was towed by the tug *CERVIA* from Ramsgate towards Southend to on 9th June. *BASILDON* is listed as a wreck off Dunkirk, although clearly she is not.

s.b. *ASHINGTON* was towed with *BASILDON,* by the tug *CERVIA,* from Ramsgate bound for Southend on 9th June 1940.

Further from Captain Miller's report, regarding *CERVIA:*
  "June 9th. Ran to Ramsgate, picked up two ex-Dunkirk sailing barges BASILDON and ASHINGTON bound for Southend. After passing NE Spit buoy a magnetic minesweeper exploded a mine alongside of us and immediately our stern barge was adrift. We went back and picked her up and continued."

The account continues with a copy of a statement re. s/s *EMPIRE COMMERCE:*
  "At about 2.30pm the drifter PLUMER came to us and spoke to us when we were approximately a mile westerly of the NE Spit buoy and requested us to go to the assistance of the

EMPIRE COMMERCE. At the same time he stated he would take over our barges, while we were assisting the EMPIRE COMMERCE."

There is no further account of what happened to *BASILDON* or *ASHINGTON*.

By now, the German forces were nearly in the outskirts of the town.

a.b. *SEINE:*
Owned by the London and Rochester Trading Co., she was taken across to France by her skipper, C. Cogger on 31st May under her own power.

'The Nine Days of Dunkirk' records:
"The motor barge SEINE under the orders of Lieutenant-Commander Filleul, on this day (3rd June) brought back 352 and on two subsequent trips brought back roughly the same number each time."

It is recorded that *SEINE* and her crew saved 793 members of the BEF in total. She returned home safely. She is not on the MNL as registered in UK. She was probably a river barge, not required to register with the board of trade.

a.b. *CABBY:*
CABBY was begun in 1925 at Strood near Rochester but not registered until 1928. She was named after the owner's wife's dog. She was the last of the full-size wooden sailing barges to be constructed by the Gill Brothers. The client went bankrupt, consequently she was not completed for three years so that another customer could be found, but Gills began to trade with her themselves, which was more profitable than boat-building. She was registered at Rochester at 76 tons and her official number was 160687 boasting a Kelvin 88hp Diesel engine. They traded as the

Rochester Barge Company, using the profits to buy land and to plant fruit. By 1924 they had all their interests in LRTC.

CABBY is listed as a 'Little Ship' and is a member of the Association, but in fact never arrived there. In 1940 she was ordered to London and loaded with drums of fresh water for the troops at Dunkirk. Instead, she was sent to the Downs to await further instructions which, coming after several days, ordered her to Brest. She was well on passage when fresh instructions returned her to Plymouth. From there, under war service, she went to Ireland, to the Clyde, to be used as a stores ship and then to the Hebrides.

m.b. *ADVANCE:*
On the National Register of Historic Ships, *ADVANCE* was a River Gravel Barge built in 1926 by Harris, P K & Sons Ltd, Appledore for the builders' merchants Devon Trading Co. Bideford, to load and transport gravel and sand from the sand bars at the mouth of the Tow and Torridge Estuary to the merchants' yards in Bideford and Barnstaple. A photograph of her working may be seen on the web site www.therollecanal.co.uk. She was only 48.07 feet in length with a depth of 4 ft. and was 20 gross tons. Only the French site records her as part of Operation Dynamo, owned by Woodward-Fisher. *ADVANCE* is now the last remaining wooden gravel barge in the Taw and Torridge estuary. She is now in the Sea Lock Basin of the Rolle Canal and can only be reached during high spring tides. Details are different on MNL.

a.b. MOUSME, (or MOUSMA):
Listed incorrectly as OD 154 *'a.b MOUSMA'*, *MOUSME* was a barge of 64 tons built in Maidstone in 1924, registered in Rochester and owned in 1934 by the London and Rochester Trading Co. She had only a Ferry engine, later installed with a Kelvin 4 engine and owned by Mrs. C. Bennett of Hammersmith, London. There is only one non-corroborated mention of her participation in the evacuation on the French website.

a.b *VALONIA:*

In the Merchant Navy list of 1934 *VALONIA* is recorded as built in East Greenwich in 1911 and registered in London, No: 132631. She was 81 tons, and possessed an auxiliary engine. Her owner was Horace Shrubsall of East Greenwich. She is listed in the Orde documents but we have no other details. She was abandoned.

s.b. *CENTAUR:*

CENTAUR, 62 tons, built in 1895 by Cann's of Harwich for William Rogers of Colchester, a typical Essex coasting barge. In 1938 she was owned by Francis & Gilders. She was requisitioned for the evacuation. To the disappointment of her crew she broke away from her tow and drove on to the pier, damaging it and herself. Appearing to spring a leak she had to return to her berth. It transpired that the water in the hold came from damage to the water carriers, not to the barge. Her cargo was transferred to s.b. *LARK.* She continued work and is today owned by the Thames Sailing Barge Trust and is now used to provide individuals with weekend cruises and longer charters. Every summer she now sails the Thames Estuary and the Essex, Suffolk and Kent rivers. She is in the list of Historic Vessels UK.

s.b. *MONARCH:*

There are two *MONARCHS* registered on MNL in 1938. One was built in 1900, 46 tons, owned by George Andrews of Murston, Sittingbourne, registered at Rochester No: 113687 and owned in 1938 by S. Ellis. This *MONARCH* is most likely to be the barge built in Sittingborne in 1905, 47 tons, registered in London in 1916 to 1938 to H. Covington & Sons of Battersea, No. 120492.

She has been mentioned once, and we have found no corroboration.

s.b. QUEEN:
A 60 ton barge built in Sittingbourne in 1906; *QUEEN* was listed for the Owen Parry Oil Mills at Colchester in 1916. By 1934 the LRTC had her and she remained with them until WW2. She was registered as owned by H. Murrell at the time of the evacuation. No other details of her have been found.

s.b. WARRIOR:
We could find no information about the part played by *WARRIOR*, except that she is listed as a wreck off Dunkirk.

s.b. QUEEN ALEXANDRA:
This old lady was built in East Greenwich in 1902, registered in London to T. Scholey & Co of East Greenwich. She was 52 tons. She was owned by Turmaine and Jones when she is said to have crossed to Dunkirk and returned home, although she is listed as a wreck off Dunkirk. We have found no details.

a.b. PLINLIMMON:
She was built in 1886 at Strood and registered in London No. 091902, a spritsail barge owned in 1938 by Captain G. Watkins of Halstow, 57 tons and 80 feet. She had a Bergius petrol engine and in 1940 was owned by Captain G. Wilkinson of Rochester. She is another barge mentioned as a wreck off Dunkirk and no corroboration has been traced.

s.b. UNIQUE:
UNIQUE is mentioned by Harvey Benham in *'Down Topsail'*. She was a 51 ton spritsail barge built in 1903 at Sittingbourne, registered in London and owned in 1938 by Wills and Pakham of Sittingbourne. Dunkirk records show her as owned by J. Churchill. There is no corroboration of her part in the evacuation. In 1942 she was sunk by a mine.

On the 3rd June the remains of the rearguard was gathering on the beach. Artilleryman W T Richardson DCM was at Bray Dunes,

Dunkirk. His commanding officer Major Phillips and his senior officer had been ordered to get themselves back to England. Major Phillips said to Artilleryman Richardson:

"We want someone to stay behind. You're a single man Mr Richardson; no doubt you'll be volunteering?"

Artilleryman Richardson replied, as was expected of him:

"Yes sir, thank you sir. I'd like to do that."

Major Phillips said:

"There aren't enough boats for everyone so you decide who goes and who stays."

Artilleryman Richardson:

"How do I do that, sir?"

"I'll leave that to you" was the reply.

They had no rations and no ammunition. Artilleryman Richardson asked the Major what he was to do about that. The Major's reply was:

"I'll leave that to you. Just do the best you can".

Mr Richardson employed the same criteria in his selection as to who went and who stayed as the Major i.e. married men could go single men stayed. 30 men stayed behind.

The last of the British army to be evacuated left on 3rd June and at 10.50 Tennant signalled Ramsey:

"Operation completed, returning to Dover".

ANOTHER 'ONE LAST STAND'

At Bastion 32, French Headquarters at Dunkirk, the mood was heavy with gloom.

There was no more fresh water; the medics had run out of bandages, communications were failing. Many Frenchmen had elected not to leave their native land, knowing that with machine gun fire on the outskirts of the town defeat was inevitable.

Ramsey sent a firm telegram to the Admiralty indicating that this must be the last night to attempt rescue.

> "I hoped and believed that last night would see us through but the French who were covering the retirement of the British rearguard had to repel a strong German attack and so were unable to send their troops to the pier in time to be embarked. We cannot leave our allies in the lurch and I call on all officers and men detailed for further evacuation tonight to let the world see that we never let down our Ally .....
>
> "After nine days of operations of a nature unprecedented in naval warfare, which followed on two weeks of intense strain, commanding officers, officers and ships companies are at the end of their tether.... If therefore evacuation has to be continued after tonight, I would emphasize in the strongest possible manner that fresh forces should be used for these operations, and any consequent delay in their execution should be accepted."

Churchill insisted we must go back for them, so the Royal Navy returned on 3rd June in an attempt to rescue as many as possible of the French rearguard.

3rd June: Winston Churchill wired Weygand and Reynaud:
> "We are coming back for your men tonight. Please ensure that all facilities are used promptly. For three hours last night many ships waited idle at great risk and danger."

Captain Halsey to his officers on the Scott class destroyer *MALCOM* as they dined:
> *"The last of the BEF was able to come off because the French held the perimeter last night. Now the French have asked us to take them off. We can't do anything else can we?"*

In spite of all they had endured a brave flotilla set out yet again. For example, the destroyer *WHITSHED* pulled out with a harmonica band playing on deck. The crew of the cabin cruiser *MERMAIDEN* comprised a sub-lieutenant, a stoker, and RAF gunner on leave and a white haired old gentleman who had a small job looking after the museum ship HMS *VICTORY*, Horatio Nelson's flagship, in Portsmouth. The motor launch *MARLBOROUGH*, previously manned by two solicitors who had had the weekend off, now carried a retired colonel and an invalided army officer. *SUN 1V*, towing fourteen launches was still skippered by Mr. Alexander, president of the company. *MTB 102* with an Admiral's flag - a striped dish cloth merrily flying again now carried Admiral Wake-Walker. A large yacht, *GULZAR*, was piloted home by a Dominican Monk. *MALCOM* sailed on her eighth trip to Dunkirk at 9.08pm with her officers wearing their bow ties and dinner jackets.

When this motley assembly arrived at the Eastern Mole weather conditions made it difficult to get the waiting French troops off. As luck would have it; the Luftwaffe was busy bombing Paris. The German army was in Dunkirk itself. The flotilla of smaller vessels followed the fast boat *MARLBOROUGH* into the harbour. In the dark, in a harbour with which no-one was familiar there were many unavoidable accidents. Nevertheless the operation continued until dawn.

The French held it at the very end to allow the final withdrawal. The last defenders had no option but to surrender to the Germans.

Dunkirk town deserted following the rearguard action [2]

German photographs of the defeat of the Allies at Dunkirk [2]

At 8 am German marines took over Bastion 32. The swastika was hauled up on the Eastern Mole at 10.20. The guns fell silent. German war correspondents photographed the remaining British and French prisoners.

Anneka, a French visitor, told us:

"I never knew my father; he had been in the rearguard. His body was found in a ditch. My mother was called to identify it eighteen months later. Imagine the condition it was in by then. My mother was just a girl. It was done to frighten us all. I do not know if they shot him in battle or in cold blood".

French troops disembarking at a port on the south coast of England.

For every seven soldiers who escaped through Dunkirk, one man was left behind as a prisoner of war (POW). The majority of these prisoners were sent on forced marches into Germany. Prisoners reported brutal treatment by their guards, including beatings, starvation, and murder. In particular, the British prisoners complained that French prisoners were given preferential treatment. Another major complaint was that German guards kicked over buckets of water that had been left at the roadside by

French civilians. Many of the prisoners were marched to the town of Trier, with the march taking as long as 20 days. Others were marched to the river Scheldt and were sent by barge to the Ruhr. The prisoners were then sent by rail to POW camps in Germany. The majority (those below the rank of corporal) then worked in German industry and agriculture for five years.

The 100,000 evacuated French troops were quickly and efficiently shuttled to camps in various parts of south-western England where they were temporarily lodged before quickly being repatriated. Approximately 100,000 Frenchmen returned to their native land from England to fight again. British ships ferried French troops to Brest, Cherbourg and other ports in Normandy and Brittany, although only about ½ of the repatriated troops were deployed against the Germans before the armistice. For many French soldiers, the Dunkirk evacuation was not a salvation, but represented only a few weeks' delay before being made POWs by the German army after their return in France.

"WARS ARE NOT WON BY EVACUATIONS"

There was an early morning fog on 4th June at 10.20 when the Swastika was hoisted on the Eastern Mole.

At 3.25am. Admiral Jean Abrial, French Naval officer in overall commander of the coast had sent his last message:
> "Enemy is reaching the outskirts. I am having the codes burnt, except the 'M' code."

Over 26,000 Frenchmen jammed the decks of the last ships to leave, the *MEDWAY QUEEN*, the destroyer *SABRE* and the liner *NORMANDIE*. The *MARACHEL FOCH* with 300 troops on board was unfortunately rammed in the fog by the minesweeper *LEDA*. The auxiliary dredger *EMILE DESCHAMPS* struck a magnetic mine off Margate and sank with 500 French troops on board. She was the 243rd vessel lost. The destroyer *SHIKARI* brought Operation Dynamo to an end on Tuesday at 3.40 am.

BBC 4th June:
> "The commander of the rearguard Major-General Harold Alexander inspected the shores of Dunkirk from a motorboat this morning to make sure no-one was left behind before boarding the last ship back to Britain."

On that afternoon Winston Churchill announced to the House of Commons that Operation Dynamo had come to its end.
> "We must be very careful not to assign to this deliverance the attributes of a victory. Wars are not won by evacuations. But there was a victory inside this deliverance, which should be noted. It was gained by the Air Force. Many of our soldiers coming back have not seen the Air Force at work; they saw only the bombers which escaped its protective attack.
>
> "Even though large tracts of Europe and many old and famous States have fallen or may fall into the grip of the

Gestapo and all the odious apparatus of Nazi rule, we shall not flag or fail. We shall go on to the end. We shall fight in France, we shall fight on the seas and oceans, we shall fight with growing confidence and growing strength in the air, we shall defend our island, whatever the cost may be. We shall fight on the beaches, we shall fight on the landing grounds, we shall fight in the fields and in the streets, we shall fight in the hills; we shall never surrender, and if, which I do not for a moment believe, this island or a large part of it were subjugated and starving, then our Empire beyond the seas, armed and guarded by the British Fleet, would carry on the struggle, until, in God's good time, the New World, with all its power and might, steps forth to the rescue and the liberation of the old."

It is said that as the House of Commons thundered in an uproar at his stirring rhetoric, Churchill muttered in a whispered aside to a colleague:

"And we'll fight them with the butt ends of broken beer bottles because that's bloody well all we've got!"

The very significant loss of military equipment abandoned in Dunkirk reinforced the financial dependence of the British government on the U.S.

Winston Churchill – 18th June 1940:

"What General Weygand called the Battle of France is over. I expect that the Battle of Britain is about to begin. Upon this battle depends the survival of Christian civilization. Upon it depends our own British life, and the long continuity of our institutions and our Empire. The whole fury and might of the enemy must very soon be turned on us.

"Hitler knows that he will have to break us in this Island or lose the war. If we can stand up to him, all Europe may be free and the life of the world may move forward into broad, sunlit uplands. But if we fail, then the whole world, including

the United States, including all that we have known and cared for, will sink into the abyss of a new Dark Age made more sinister, and perhaps more protracted, by the lights of perverted science.

"Let us therefore brace ourselves to our duties, and so bear ourselves that if the British Empire and its Commonwealth last for a thousand years, men will still say, 'This was their finest hour'."

From 27th May to the 4th June 1940, a staggering total of 338,226 soldiers were rescued from either death or imprisonment by the Germans. As well as the Naval ships they came in twos and threes, or a dozen here, two dozen there, by ad-hoc civilian crews pulled together from London and the southern ports, not, as myth would have it, enthusiastic civilians, although there were a few of those, but merchant seamen, with soldiers or Royal Navy personnel aboard. Through the courage of the men of the army, the air force, the navy and the Merchant navy, semi retired Admirals to lads of 14 years, the BEF and part of the French force, were given the opportunity to regroup, re-arm and fight again.

There is no doubt that had it not been for the success of Operation Dynamo in saving the core of the British Army, the history of Britain for the past 70 years would have been very different.

Following the withdrawal and the decision to reserve our fighter aircraft for the defence of Britain, the War Cabinet evolved a plan for a Franco-British Unity, including plans for common citizenship and joint defence, financial and economic policy. It was hoped that this offer would help Reynaud, the French Prime Minister to move his government to Africa to carry on active French involvement in the war.

The French rejected the plan, with Reynaud resigning on 16th June.

Norman Brook:
> "If it had not been for Winston anything might have happened after Dunkirk. While he was there bargaining with Hitler was out of the question, a separate peace unthinkable."

The 'Miracle of Dunkirk' gave Churchill just what was needed to swell the hearts of the people with pride and determination, for indeed we had shown that for us, the British, anything was possible.

Admiral Ramsey received countless letters of gratitude. Mrs. S. Woodcock:
> ".. after reading .. of your wonderful feat re Dunkirk I feel I must send you a personal message to thank you. My son was one of the lucky ones to escape from there. I have not seen him but he is somewhere in England and that is good enough. My youngest boy John died of wounds received in Norway on April 26th...."

Railway inspector Richard Butcher:
> "When the men arrived back from Dunkirk I saw sparks flying along the London-Dover line as broken men pitched their weapons out of the window."

The Local Defence Volunteers, remembered now as 'Dad's Army', in 1940 used to training with broom handles or pitchforks, scoured the tracks collecting what they could for their own use when the Germans came. Some soldiers deserted after contacting their families. The returning men, bandaged, weary, with incomplete or ripped uniforms had expected angry faces, hostile crowds. But most were greeted as heroes as they staggered off the trains bringing them away from the south coast.

They chalked the letters BEF on their helmets or had unofficial shoulder badges made up. They were given hugs and kisses along with the cups of tea or cocoa, sandwiches, even precious chocolate.

Wounded soldiers returning to hugs and kisses, cups of hot tea, blankets... the BEF were coming home

It was the beginning of building morale and re-forming the army after the terrible defeat they had suffered. The British people, both service personnel and civilians, were inspired by this incredible event. It was not just the eloquent, defying speeches of Winston

Churchill or the propaganda machine that created this feeling – it was the effect of seeing courage above and beyond the call of duty, the knowledge that we were alone but not defeated, that we were defending our very homes, and the men had come back to do it. And it was not just soldiers who had made this great event happen, but civilians, volunteers, and the women who welcomed them home with such love and gratitude. In this case civilians rushed to rescue an army, not the usual way round. From that day in 1940 examples of ordinary people sticking together to overcome potential disaster is called 'The Dunkirk Spirit'. The nine days of Dunkirk became the stuff of legend.

German photograph of Dunkirk following Operation Dynamo

Despite the success of the operation, all the heavy equipment and vehicles had to be abandoned. Left behind in France were 2,472 heavy guns, 11,000 machine guns, 700 tanks, almost 43,500 cars & lorries and 20,500 motorcycles; also abandoned were 377,000 tons of stores, more than 68,000 tons of ammunition and 147,000 tons of fuel. The 30,000-40,000 troops left behind in the Dunkirk pocket were taken prisoner, mostly French and a few British.

The Royal Navy's most significant losses in the operation were six destroyers, the *GRAFTON, GRENADE, WAKEFUL, BASILISK, HAVANT* and *KEITH*.

The French lost three destroyers, the *BOURRASQUE, SIROCCO* and *LE FOUDROYANT*. Over 200 of the Allied sea craft were sunk, with an equal number damaged. The Royal Navy claimed the destruction of 35 Luftwaffe aircraft and damage to a further 21 from ships gunfire.

Winston Churchill revealed in his volumes on World War II that the Royal Air Force (RAF) played a most important role protecting the retreating troops from the Luftwaffe. Churchill also said that the sand on the beach softened the explosions from the German bombs.

Between 26th May and 4th June, the RAF flew a total of 4,822 sorties over Dunkirk. Fortunately for the BEF, bad weather kept the Luftwaffe grounded for much of operation thus helping to reduce the losses.

Estimates of aircraft losses during the operation vary significantly. The losses of British aircraft vary between 106 and 177 and those of German between 135 and 240.

However, most of the dogfights took place far from the beaches and the retreating troops were largely unaware of this vital assistance. As a result, many British soldiers bitterly accused the airmen of doing nothing to help.

Robert Jackson 1974:
"They call Dunkirk a great defeat and I suppose it was in reality. But in a sense there was a victory because for three weeks we held at bay the best the German army could throw at us. And what were we?
"For the most part young lads with rifles, that was all."

Peter Hadley, BEF soldier:
"The amazing welcome that we received was more suited to a victory parade than the return of a vanquished army."

JB Priestly, 5th June 1940:
> "Here at Dunkirk is another English Epic and to my mind what was most characteristically English about it – so typical of us – so absurd yet so grand and gallant that you hardly know whether to laugh or cry ..."

Nella Last, Barrow in Furness June 1940:
> "I felt everything was worthwhile. And I felt glad that I was of the same race as the resuers and rescued."

Marshal Dowding in a letter to Winston Churchill:
> "Well now it is England against Germany and I don't envy them the job."

General Field Marshall Gerd von Rumstedt:
> "This was one of the great turning points of the war"

The escape of the BEF was a strategic disaster for the Germans. What should have been an operational triumph evolved into a defeat. If the BEF had been annihilated that spring, it is difficult to see how Britain could have continued to fight: and with Britain out of the battle it is even more difficult to see how America and Stalin's Russia could have allied to challenge Hitler.

DANGEROUS WORK

John White of the Society for Sailing Barge Research has recorded some interesting tales of Whitstable barges' adventures during the war.

Built 1895 at Whitstable for Whitstable Shipping Company, *DULUTH* was a Spritsail barge of 57 registered Tons. The company was later owned by Daniel Brothers of Whitstable. *DULUTH* sank near the Mid-Shoebury Buoy 10th May 1942 after running over the wreck of a mined steamer. It was the second loss for Daniel Brothers that year. Her Skipper Albert Fryer, had been aboard *H.K.D.* when she was also mined in January 1942.

MAJOR built 1897 at Harwich as a boomie of 67 tons for Groom's was requisitioned as a munitions barge during WW2. She was returned in a sorry state but was used by her owners to Daniel Brothers until 1962.

Another Daniel Brothers barge *THOMAS AND FRANCES* was stripped of most of her gear in 1939 for possible use as a harbour block ship before being laid up by 1944 at Whitstable and cannibalised to keep others in the fleet working. She was towed as a hulk at Murston Quay to London in 1951 for the Festival of Britain as part of a fireworks display and was finally burnt.

WHY NOT?, 38 Registered tons, Built 1866 at Faversham by J Usher of Faversham for his own use, was also owned by Daniel Brothers and in 1938 lay as a wreck at Rosherville, Northfleet, and had a most interesting and chequered life as a hulk. Sometime in WW2 a plane from No. 63 R.A.F. Training Squadron based at Joyce Green, flying very low over Long Reach crashed onto her deck. The pilot was killed and the observer injured. *WHY NOT?* was badly damaged. A tug from the Cory Company was nearby and lashed her alongside to tow her to the shore where she was beached. Although now virtually hulked someone made minor modifications to her hold and lived aboard her.

Other barges and their crews on war work led dangerous lives. The list is by no means complete.

AILSA, 67 tons built in 1898 at Deptford for Goldsmiths of London hit a mine by Whitaker Spit and sank, 13th Jan 1943. Her crew were saved.

VICTOR, 56 tons, was built by Horace Shrubsall at the Dock End Yard, Ipswich in 1895 for Owen Parry or Edward Hibbs of Brightlingsea, according to which account we read. In 1938 she was owned by LRTC. Until the Second World War she collected linseed from farms around the East Coast and took it to Owen Parry's Mill in Colchester returning to London with the oil in barrels. It is thought that this cargo may have in large part contributed to her excellent condition. In 1926 Felix Mallett, one of the most renowned skippers of his generation with distinguished service in both world wars, left *GRETA*, owned by London & Rochester Shipping Co, to skipper *VICTOR*. In 1932 she was valued at £450 when the Owen Parry Company was bought by London & Rochester Trading Co. *VICTOR's* war work included working out of Chatham dock during the war loading munitions. Working during the night she transferred torpedoes and shells to cruisers, corvettes and destroyers. She survived a bomb that directly hit and completely destroyed the lighter she was lying alongside. The last sailing barge to be decommissioned in 1947 she was towed to Brightlingsea along with s.b. *CHEIFTAN*, who sank, being towed too fast. *VICTOR* survived this danger also and in the 50's she was converted to a motor barge and traded for the London & Rochester Company on the Medway until sold in 1964, again for £450. She represented Suffolk and the Lord Lieutenant of Suffolk in 2012, during the Thames river pageant celebrating the Diamond Jubilee of Queen Elizabeth II, skippered by David (Wes) Westwood.

ALARIC, 73 tons built 1901 at Sandwich as *SHAMROCK* for Wm Co., owned in 1938 by Francis and Gilders, was in the Whitaker Channel on 12th March 1943, skippered by Harry Eves and his son Adam. At 8.30am the barge was strafed by machine gun fire from six German Fighters. Harry died from his wounds, although Adam, only scratched, turned the barge around to make for the safety of Burnham on Crouch.

s.b. *RESOLUTE* 60 tons, built in 1903 and owned by Horlocks of Mistley, on 24th January 1943 hit a mine in the estuary of the River Crouch. The barge sank taking with it the mate although the skipper was picked up from the sea by rescue units.

a.b. *CASTANET a* Colchester owned barge of 46 tons, built in 1897 in Ipswich for Goldsmiths of London struck the wreck of the ss *SKAGERAK* in the River Orwell on 6th March 1943, then owned by Francis and Gilders. Much of her cargo of wheat was saved. Her sailing gear was recovered a month later by an Ipswich barge, *GENERAL JACKSON,* from Pin Mill where *CASTANET* lay and was eventually hulked before being swept across the river to Levington Creek during the gale and flood of 31st January/1st February 1953.

Of other LRTC barges, *KNOWLES* like *ALDERMAN* was lost on the Clyde. *ENCHANTRESS* was lost during the blitz whilst in the London Docks, when Rank's flour mill fell on top of her. Dramatically, *WOODHAM COURT, HERBERT* and *KINGFISHER* were all lying on the Lower Mooring off Strood Dock and were destroyed when a German F.W. 190 was shot down.

BANKSIDE was registered in London, No: 112749. Built in 1900 at Milton-next-Sittingbourne, in 1916 she was owned by Wakely Brothers of Lambeth. She was then 52 tons, but was rebuilt to 60 tons in 1927 and by 1934 was part of the Shrubsall of East Greenwich fleet. In 1938 she was bought by Colonel Bingham and worked with Francis and Gilders fleet. *BANKSIDE* was laden with flour when she hit a mine off Maplin Sands on 19th December 1942 at 7.30am and broke in two. Trapped in the wreckage, the skipper went down with her. The rear end stayed afloat for a short period that allowed a fishing smack to close in and pick up the first mate still plastered with wet flour following the explosion when he was taken to hospital at Burnham on Crouch.

BIJOU was built in Ipswich in 1906, displacing 79 tons and originally named *HILDA*. Sold to P. Verheyden of Dunkirk she was re-named *GRAVELINES II*. In 1912 she was bought back but as there was another barge named *HILDA* she was re-named again after Mrs. William Paul's dog. On 3rd July 1940, her skipper was Harold Smy. She was set on fire during an incendiary bomb raid on Mistley: her mooring line burnt and she floated out beyond the reach of fire engines and burnt out. Much of her gear was rescued and brought back to Ipswich to do a turn on some other barge.

ROSME, was owned by the London and Rochester Trading Co. She was 67 tons and built in 1927 in Maidstone. She struck a mine off Maplin Sand during the war. Skipper Harold Smy managed to save his mate, who was below at the time, and was later awarded the British Empire Medal. When he retired in 1965 he was master of LRTC's *WYVENHOE*.

s.b. EDME, official No: 105425, was built of wood at Harwich in 1898 at 50 tons by Cann for F.W.Horlock of Mistley. She was de-rigged for use as a lighter in 1949 by Brown & Co. Although mentioned on one list as a Dunkirk Little Ship we have found no other corroboration. She underwent lengthy restoration at Maldon before being bought by the Harman-Harrison Consortium and re-rigged as bowsprit barge 1992.

Now owned by the *EDME* Consortium she still has no engine and is based at St.Osyth.

a.b. *ALDERMAN:*
Built in 1905 in London, registered at Harwich, *ALDERMAN* was 65 tons according to the Merchant Navy list of 1916 when owned by John B Groom of Harwich. Some of Groom's barges, including *ALDERMAN* were taken over by the London and Rochester Trading Company in 1924.

The only mention found of her trading days is that of Frank Carr when in 1928 she was lying in the Gore, skippered by Captain Flory. He writes:
"Shortly before midnight the ALDERMAN sailed, her skipper believing that if he got down to Margate he might find the wind going round into the sou'west and giving him a chance to slip across to Dunkirk".

Evidently she was one of several barges who traded regularly with the continent. Her final visit to a port where her crew doubtless had made many friends in many portside haunts (also described in colourful detail by Carr) must have been heart-wrenching for them. Although mentioned in a French list, we found no detailed account of any part she may have played in Operation Dynamo, but she later went up to the Clyde, acting as a lighter and transporting military stores and mail to the Cunarders *QUEEN MARY* and *QUEEN ELIZABETH* which were working as transatlantic troop ships. *ALDERMAN* was lost while in the Clyde on war service.

DOVER CASTLE

Britons on the cliffs at Dover forced Caesar's Roman army to land further north at Walmer in 43 AD. Within seven years a lighthouse had been erected on the cliff which still stands today. The grand castle was built by William the Conqueror in 11th century and almost certainly continually garrisoned for 2,000 years. The mediaeval defences were enlarged during the 1740's, the tunnels constructed during the Napoleonic wars in 1797 when there were 2,000 men barracked in two miles of tunnel. During WWII a further two miles were constructed, serving as a combined headquarters and hospital. The complex was never bombed, for two reasons. It served as a landmark for enemy 'planes flying in over the channel, but significantly the castle's iconic reputation made Hitler determined that *he* would occupy the site when 'Operation Sealion', his conquest of Britain was achieved.

Operations room for Operation Dynamo, Dover Castle*

Auxiliary Territorial Service plotter:

"Were we afraid? Well of course, to some extent, but although us girls didn't discuss it. I think being where we were, in that great fortress which had stood for 1,000 years, working in the white cliffs of Dover, among colleagues prepared to give their lives, well it was all so solid, so British, that we didn't think about being afraid. On the first day we asked to work 24 hour shifts, it was obviously going to be required. Those manning the telephone or the plotters just stepped over the sleeping bodies on the floor. The Vice-Admiral and his number two had little cots in two small rooms, alcoves really, where they could snatch sleep when exhaustion overtook them. There was a washroom and fairly primitive toilet facilities. We managed."

St. Mary in Castro, next to the Roman lighthouse is the garrison church of forces based at Dover Castle. During two weeks in May/June 1940 the funerals and burials of 140 soldiers, the men coming back from France with un-dressed wounds, lost limbs, blood loss, shock or dying of heart attacks caused by terror and exhaustion, took place there.

St. Mary in Castro *

Air raids, troop movements, the chaos caused by families moving away from the south of England prevented mourners from attending most of them. The Senior Chaplain conducted the services; his wife attended every one, grieving for each in place of mothers, sisters, fathers or brothers, wives and children - one woman grieving for 140 men. Duty calling, you see, each person giving all they could give.

Throughout World War II Dover suffered severe shelling, becoming known as 'Hellfire Corner'. During the nine day period 200,000 troops came through Dover. The Southern Railway laid on a total of 327 special trains, which cleared 180,982 troops. 4,500 casualties were treated at the town's Buckland Hospital and all but 50 of these seriously ill men were saved.

Battlement defences at Dover Castle *

The rescue of the British troops at Dunkirk provided a psychological boost to British morale; to the country at large it was spun as a major victory. While the British Army had lost a great deal of its equipment and vehicles in France, it still had most of its soldiers and was able to assign them to the defence of Britain. Once the threat of invasion receded, they were transferred overseas to the Middle East and other theatres and also provided the nucleus of the army that returned to France in 1944.

Bertram Ramsey continued to play an important part in the strategy and operation of World War II. In 1945 he was killed in an air crash near Paris. Honours included: Knight Commander of the Order of the Bath: Knight Commander of the Order of the British Empire: Member of the Royal Victorian Order: Mentioned in Despatches (2): Légion d'honneur (France): Legion of Merit (United States): Order of Ushakov (USSR).

OPERATION ARIEL
From 'Whereabouts Unknown' by Tim Lynch

The evacuation of the last of the infantry divisions responsible for lines of communication took place from Normandy ports. 'Operation Ariel', was in full swing from 14th June 1940. Untrained troops of the Labour Divisions were sacrificed to save an army, many eventually listed as 'Whereabouts Unknown'.

There were no maps of the terrain available to officers trying to organise their men who were many miles south of Dunkirk. These men were on their own and on the run. Their experiences were appalling, but strengthened the resolve of many that the invading armies should not take Britain.

While trying to cross a river, men of the Kings Own Yorkshire Light Infantry saw the French blow the bridge in front of them. Those trying to swim across were swept away and lost in the strong current.

Flowers:
> *"I was running. When I was about seventy yards away it just blew up: I can see it now; there were a series of small explosions along the length of the bridge. I was never a boy after that. It looks pretty certain to me that the French sacrificed us".*

Brigadier (Acting Major General) A. B. Beauman, Commander of the Cherbourg area:
> *"I should hesitate to blame the French for blowing the bridge ... on this occasion ... stringent orders had been issued by the French High Command that regardless of the local situation bridges were to be blown as soon as the enemy approached them ... the French officer in charge had justification for his action".*

Beauman:
> "Six of a French Senegalese regiment were captured and made to sit at tables outside the village café. Each one was shot in the back of the head and as his head fell forwards it was snatched back and his throat slit."

On 17th June, Junkers Ju88 bombers of Kampfgeschwader 30 found the *LANCASTRIA*, Cunard's 16,243 ton luxury liner as it lay off St. Nazaire. It was estimated that almost 9,000 soldiers and refugees were crowded onto the ship. Chief Officer Harry Grattidge, *LANCASTRIA's* second in command:
> "The smoke drifted and parted and we saw the most terrible sight the LANCASTRIA could offer; the mess of blood and oil and splintered woodwork that littered the deck and the furious white core of water that came roaring from the bottom of the ship in Number 4 hold. I took the megaphone, hearing my voice booming out strangely over the dying ship. 'Clear away the boats now ... your attention please ... clear away the boats now'. The LANCASTRIA quaked under my feet, a last gesture of farewell".

There was panic and chaos. In blind panic people struggled to survive as German planes returned to mercilessly strafe the sinking ship with machine gun fire. Those who dived under water to escape the clutches of drowning men without lifejackets carried feelings of guilt for the rest off their lives. As many as 6,000 lives were lost in the space of a minute.

Winston Churchill:
> "I forbade it's (the LANCASTRIA) publication. The newspapers have got quite enough disaster for today at least. I had intended to release the news a few days later, but events crowded upon us so black and so quickly that I forgot to lift the ban, and it was some years before the knowledge of this horror became public".

General Sir Edward Spiers, flying back from Paris saw another ship on the same day:

"... suddenly I beheld a terrible sight. A great ship was lying on her side, sinking. Hundreds of tiny figures could be seen in the water. It was the CHAMPLAIN, with two thousand British troops on board. We cut across Brittany. We were flying low and the entire countryside seemed to be on fire for there was smoke everywhere. I thought it was the Germans burning villages but I was told later they were British Army dumps being destroyed".

The last of the men returning with Operation Ariel arrived in Plymouth on 25th June. As the men marched from the docks:

"There were thousands of women waiting for us. The women lined the two sides of the narrow corridor which had formed through which we would have to march wanting to know if we had seen their husbands, sons and boyfriends while on our way to the coast in France, They held out photographs of their missing loved ones and pleaded with us for news. It was a harrowing, unbelievably sad and grief-stricken struggle for us to get through them and up to the station".

The men did not even know the fate of their closest friends. By the time the last men returned from France the novelty of 'The Miracle of Dunkirk' had already worn off. For most of these last few the homecoming was an anti-climax. They travelled alone or in groups to stations where no-one knew or cared what they had been through. Dunkirk was just a memory and these men were not the fighting heroes people had heard so much about, they were the 'useless mouths' of the Lines of Communication. Beauman had great difficulty in submitting recommendations for awards for his men. Throughout the summer and autumn of 1940 other men continued to make their way home after being on the run in France for months. The fate of thousands was never known.

THE GERMANS ARE COMING

As you look up to the castle at Dover you can see two archways in the cliff, the entrance to four miles of tunnels. Stand on the balcony afforded by those two tunnel entrances: look down on to the port of Dover, does your inner eye see the inner and outer harbours guarded by stout walls and towers, full of ships, as Vice-Admiral Ramsey saw them in June, 1940? Do you see the decks heaving with men, the exhausted, and the wounded?

Do you see the water outside the harbour crowded with destroyers, tugs, small boats all trying to manoeuvre without crashing into each other, some broken, all grimy, all simply relieved to be back home?

Imagine Ramsey and his officers looking across the water to where you can see France in the morning sun, the smoke still rising from the burning channel ports and the British ships that have not made it home, that are still on fire in the channel. Imagine their thoughts as they know that their German counterparts, led by Hermann Goering are standing on the other side looking back at the cliffs of Dover.

These two legendary men gazed at each other across the 20 miles of grey water. What were their thoughts? Eager anticipation by the one, trepidation on the part of the other, for the Germans were coming. The only question was 'When'?

The Nazi forces had blanketed other European countries; they had parachuted into mountain areas, ground forces had marched over the countryside, tanks had rolled unstoppably forward, a detachment of troops occupied every village, the Luftwaffe bombed defenceless terrified civilians in cities. It was completely successful. Britain was next.

Another lady told us how afraid everybody was in Ramsgate in 1940:

> *"Everybody was afraid. You could hear the noise of the 'planes and the guns in France. Some of the long range guns could fire almost onto the beach. Everyone knew the invasion was coming and the army was in disarray. We got everyone away from Hastings within the week. Only about 1,000 people stayed behind. You couldn't live there, there was nothing working. You could hear the guns in France, the red glow that we were told were the French ports burning. Shells from the German big guns landed just off the shore. The 'planes overhead added to the noise that went on and on for days".*

Barbara:

Half a million children were evacuated from big cities – most from London - to the countryside during 1939 and 1940. It was an extraordinary mass movement. Families often remained apart for all of the six years. Children were stuffed into trains and sent all over the country. Thames pleasure steamers loaded with children disembarked them into East Anglian ports.

The beaches where I had played were guarded by barbed wire. I, just a toddler, was lucky to travel with my mother from Hastings, on trains packed with soldiers coming back from Dunkirk in June, 1940. The memory has never left me of travelling in the dark, blacked out trains, the smell of the damp khaki coats, Will's Woodbine's smoked behind the hands, the gentle way those men treated my mother and me.

My mother salvaged nothing from our flat but what she could carry, a suitcase, our gas masks and me. The families who took in evacuees were paid 5/- a week 25p in today's money, for each child. People chose the children they liked the look of. Being the last to be chosen, they say, has scarred people for life! We had to go. Everyone knew the Germans were coming".

A. R. P.

HOUSEHOLDER'S
AIR RAID PRECAUTIONS CHART

Illustrating Home Office Instructions

HOW TO MAKE A ROOM GAS-PROOF

Details at a Glance

Inexpensive Materials

COMPLETE DIAGRAM FOR HOME CONSTRUCTION

Articles Recommended for Emergency • Choice of Room

What to do in a Raid

3d.

COPYRIGHT

Published by JORDAN & SONS, LIMITED, 116 CHANCERY LANE, LONDON, W.C.2
Tel.: HOLBORN 0434

ARTICLES RECOMMENDED TO BE IN YOUR REFUGE ROOM AT A TIME OF EMERGENCY

The undermentioned items are articles which are probably possessed already or can be collected beforehand.

1—String, hammer and nails, scissors.
2—Gummed paper and adhesive tape.
3—Pot of paste, or gum for pasting paper over cracks and window panes. Paste can be made from flour and water boiled with a few cloves put in to keep it fresh. For windows, thin sheets of transparent or translucent non-inflammable material (commonly used for wrapping purposes) can be used. Requires cellulose lacquer to stick down.
4—Candles, matches, lamp or electric handlamp. Needles, cotton and thread, material to protect the windows, e.g. old newspaper and brown paper, transparent wrapping material, or, failing this, some fabric material such as linen from old pillow cases or mosquito netting. A few tins or jars with air tight lids for storing food.
5—Bottle of disinfectant, clean rags. Box of First-Aid supplies, containing a few bandages, small packet of boracic lint, cotton wool, some safety pins, a second pair of scissors, a bottle of smelling salts, sal volatile, at least one pair of dark lens glasses (non-inflammable).

On an emergency arising the undermentioned articles should be placed in the Refuge Room in addition to those already mentioned.

A **Roll Call List** of all who should be present. This applies particularly to office premises, or if the room is to be shared by neighbours.

6—**Gas Masks** for all, with owners name on box. Puncture outfit for mending masks might be useful.
7—A food chest of some kind (air-tight tins or jars will do) as a precaution against contact with gas. Tinned food, tin-opener, corkscrew.
8—Plenty of water for drinking, washing and for damping the door blanket.
9—Plates, cups, knives, forks, etc.
10—Flasks for hot tea or coffee.
11—Paper pulp for re-sealing cracks, etc. (wet newspaper)
12—Sand and water for fire emergency, or a fire extinguisher, and a simple hand pump if possible.
13—Shovel (long handle best), tables and chairs, washhand-stand, or basin, soap, towels, etc.
14—A screen, for privacy, chamber pots, toilet paper, disinfectant.
15—Spare blankets or rugs for re-sealing the window if it should be blown in. Mattresses to lie on. Overcoats, blankets, rugs and warm coverings.
16—Mackintoshes, goloshes, gum boots (useful for outside reconnaissance after raid).
17—Wireless set (a battery best as electric current might fail), gramophone with records.
18—Books, writing materials, toys. Table in corner against inner wall. "When raid overhead, good place under table."

WHEN WARNING OF A RAID IS GIVEN.

FIRST
    Close all windows and doors in rest of house. Put out fires. Turn off gas. Electric light may be used.

SECOND
    Call the Roll and be certain that everyone who should be in the room is present.

THIRD
Seal the entrance to the room.

Rest quietly to save Oxygen.

NO SMOKING.

**10, DOWNING STREET,
WHITEHALL.**

O N what may be the eve of an attempted invasion or battle for our native land, the Prime Minister desires to impress upon all persons holding responsible positions in the Government, in the Fighting Services, or in the Civil Departments, their duty to maintain a spirit of alert and confident energy. While every precaution must be taken that time and means afford, there are no grounds for supposing that more German troops can be landed in this country, either from the air or across the sea, than can be destroyed or captured by the strong forces at present under arms. The Royal Air Force is in excellent order and at the highest strength it has yet attained. The German Navy was never so weak, nor the British Army at home so strong as now. The Prime Minister expects all His Majesty's servants in high places to set an example of steadiness and resolution. They should check and rebuke expressions of loose and ill-digested opinion in their circles, or by their subordinates. They should not hesitate to report, or if necessary remove, any officers or officials who are found to be consciously exercising a disturbing or depressing influence, and whose talk is calculated to spread alarm and despondency. Thus alone will they be worthy of the fighting men, who in the air, on the sea, and on land, have already met the enemy without any sense of being out-matched in martial qualities.

Winston S. Churchill

4th July, 1940.

Information leaflets were issued to the civilian population. Posters warned 'CARELESS TALK COSTS LIVES'. There were hasty preparations for the evacuation of children from the areas most in danger.

Italy, Germany's Axis partner had used Mustard Gas in Abyssinia in 1936. Afraid that the gas would be used in the coming invasion everyone in England was issued with a gas mask.

By the first week of September 1940 there were a growing number of enemy barges assembling at the Channel ports – Dunkirk, Calais Ostend, Le Havre, Flushing and Ostend. Other vessels, large and small were joining them. Airfields near the Pas De Calais were filling up with assembling bombers and dive-bombers.

Operation Sealion, the planned invasion of England, was to be in August 1940; it was put off to 8th and 10th September the dates when moon and tide would be favourable for a landing. Goering confidently promised his Luftwaffe would easily defeat the Royal Air Force. On 3rd September the German High Command proposed postponing Sealion again and on 15th launched a major attack to destroy the RAF. Thanks to the courage of 'the few'; as Churchill describes them, they failed to do so. The Germans lost twice as many planes as the RAF. Sealion was postponed indefinitely on the 17th and that effectively signalled its end.

On 28th June, the Luftwaffe had bombed undefended Jersey and Guernsey, killing 44 people. On 30th June Luftwaffe personnel took control of Guernsey airfield. There they met the chief of police, who informed them that the islands were undefended. The German flag was raised on 1st July 1940.

Jersey also surrendered on 1st July and German soldiers were swiftly stationed there. Sybil Hathaway, the Dame of Sark, received German officers on 2nd July.

A small garrison was set up on Alderney, but not on little Herm, the smallest of the islands.

There was now a curfew between 11pm and 5am. ID cards were mandatory. Wirelesses were banned and all British-born Islanders were deported to Germany.

A register of Jewish people was created and all Jewish businesses had to publicly identify themselves. Many Jews were deported to concentration camps. Cars were requisitioned and the sale of spirits was banned: there followed serious food shortages as Germans controlled the food grown by farmers and anything caught by fishermen. Anyone caught trying to escape to mainland Britain was imprisoned often in concentration camps, or shot.

Four concentration camps were built on Alderney - the only ones on British territory. Alderney became the most heavily fortified of the islands, using local slave labour.

Sarah Blake, 'The Postmistress':
"By the autumn bombs were falling on Coventry, London, Kent. Sleek metal pellets like the blunt tipped ends of pencils aimed down upon hedgerow and thatch. In American 'Life Magazine' the children of Coventry were pictured... 'unafraid there in the ditch dug for safety (the children) looked up...the boy with no expression ...the collar of his jacket fastened with a safety pin'. It asked *'Would England stand? Their tanks and trucks, their guns, hulked useless on the other side of the channel where they had left them'"?*

But defeat, for defeat it was, became refusal to be defeated. If 80 year old wooden sailing boats could be part of a mission to save an army, why not the cannons at the British Museum? So they hauled them down to the Thames to have something to defend London against a water born invasion. In the end the relentless bombing that started in September became a weapon to defeat Hitler because as Londoners emerged from the railway stations turned into air-raid shelters, the cellars, the bridges that gave them night shelter they greeted the autumn sun with smiles, realising that they could survive this. Their men had toughed it out in France, so could they. Besides the King and Queen were staying, and the little princesses, there was a job to be done.

Later, General Brook:
> "Had the BEF not returned to this country it is hard to see how the army could have recovered from the blow."

It was hard but not impossible to re-equip the army with the colossal losses of vehicles, equipment and ordnance in France. The trained British troops that were rescued would have been irreplaceable.

The French held Dunkirk to the very end to allow the final withdrawal, when the town finally surrendered to the Germans there were about 35,000 Allied prisoners taken, mostly French.

No doubt, had it not been for the success of Operation Dynamo in saving the core of the British Army, the history of Britain for the past 70 years would have been very different. Before the operation was completed, the prognosis had been gloomy, with Winston Churchill warning the House of Commons to expect *"hard and heavy tidings"*. Subsequently, Churchill referred to the outcome as a *"miracle",* and the British press presented the evacuation as a *"disaster turned to triumph"* so successfully that Churchill had to remind the country, in a speech to the House of Commons on 4th June, that:
> *"we must be very careful not to assign to this deliverance the attributes of a victory."*

Nevertheless, exhortations to the "Dunkirk spirit", a phrase used to describe the tendency of the British public to pull together and overcome times of adversity, are still heard in Britain today.

THE 50th ANNIVERSARY 1990

Wednesday 23rd May The Duke of Edinburgh inspects the fleet *

On deck *

CABBY, PUDGE and *ENA* joined the flotilla of 'Little Ships of Dunkirk' in 1990, on the 50th anniversary of the evacuation. There were still plenty of survivors then, or their wives, both French and English. Theirs are many of the stories recorded here.

On Thursday 24th May 1990 The gates of the Wellington dock opened and the 78 Little Ships flotilla set sail from Dover towards Dunkirk under light breezes force 3 – 4, clearing the Harbour at 11.10 while the crowds on either side of the lock cheered, with a Klaxon fog horn adding to the din. Outside the harbour we formed a column of 19 rows, 4 abreast, attended by H.M.S. *ALACRITY* and several other Naval vessels including combined services yacht *SABRE* and the Dover lifeboat, plus a collection of spectator boats, including the "New" paddle steamer *WAVERLY*. The original was sunk at Dunkirk.

John recorded:
> *"It is strange how emotion catches you out. The sight of 200 vessels moving purposefully towards France almost brought tears."*

As we approached the traffic separation zones the rear half of the formation, previously 4 abreast, came up to form lines of eight abreast, with barges and *BLUEBIRD II* bringing up the rear. *HMS ALACRITY* was to the North of the flotilla advising approaching shipping on how to avoid the convoy. Once we were clear to the North she crossed our bows at speed and spoke to the vessels to the south which were approaching the convoy.

There is one-way traffic for ships going East/west (or vice-versa along the English Channel. Small boats crossing North Sea traffic lanes must cross at right angles as quickly as possible to keep out of the way. At the briefing this was likened to shepherding 75 old ladies across a busy road, all holding hands.

ENA and CABBY from PUDGE, *leaving Dover* *

Tony:
> "ENA, PUDGE and CABBY took up station to the rear of the convoy. On board PUDGE we felt very sorry for the crews of the Little Ships who were taking quite a battering. Some of our crew were feeling the worse for wear."

A lone Spitfire made several low passes over the fleet in salute.

The dangers faced by the rescuers in 1940 can be estimated by part of the log kept during our own crossing despite the shepherding. It details a dozen little ships that had to be towed to harbour, crews evacuated, because of injury of engine failure. Within 15 minutes small *MONARCH* turned back in distress.

PUDGE's log:
> "13.40 ELIZABETH BREEN slowing down. Conditions too hard. Convoy now clear of shipping lanes and turning North off Calais, proceeding along French coast. Flag officer to convoy. 'slow down ½ knot'. Heavy swell. The main disadvantage we found of the shorter course Z was the rolling swell occasioned by the waves hitting the shoreline and coming back. Lots of seasickness on our barge, which is a large, reasonable stable vessel. Goodness knows what is going on smaller boats. L'ORANGE stopped both engines, drifting, relying on outboard.
>
> "DAPHNE reports engine failure. WENDY KEN instructed to assist. Refuses, apology, two crew very sick. Conditions very bad on small ships. Lifeboat to go. JOCKETTE in tow by ROSE HARTY.
>
> "ARKION shipping water. Lifeboat preparing to go alongside her.
>
> "BLUEBIRD II suggests Little Ships who are desperate could go into Port West and through the channel. (Remember this option was no longer available in 1940. It had been destroyed and blocked by sunken vessels.) No takers, stubborn little blighters!

"TANTALUS engine give up completely. She is taken in tow. Meanwhile PUDGE, with engine and sail, is blistering along, making 7 knots. ENA has some problem, falls behind her section. MARDA running on one engine, 'request permission to enter Port West'. Affirmative.

"Waves are now very high, troughs very low. Average 7 feet, some are twelve feet. There must be misery among the small craft. BREDA both engines failed. Poor radio contact. TERIFA cannot restart engine, urgently requests assistance into harbour. THELMA, BREDA and WINDSONG all in trouble. GAY VENTURE radios 'Only one engine'. Poor radio contact, messages broken up. Walmin lifeboat takes DAPHNE in tow. ELIZABETH GREEN, WENDY KEN, ARKION TANTALUS, GAY VENTURE and LADY HAIG all reporting difficulties due to the increased wind force. Our section going in. ENA has lost 2 of her 6 cylinders.

"PUDGE reports engine failure. Flag requests shelter of lock for the little vessels and queries the order for 2nd class, saying 'Dirty great barge needs a lot of help from harbour authorities'.

"17.45: CABBY now under port control, going in. BLUEBIRD II and PUDGE to follow. ENA has lost two of her six cylinders. Flag radios to ENA 'Ensure PUDGE has precedence before CATCHALOT for latters own safety'. CATCHALOT replies haughtily 'Thank you I *am* familiar with the habits of barges'.

"The problem is is going to be stopping PUDGE, with the wind up her transom and no engine. She is taken in tow by the French tug ENTREPRENANT and are pulled at great speed then cast off as she approached the lock gates resulting in an almighty crash and splintering of wood as we crash into the outer wall. Two crew members are holding inadequate fenders of over the bow until yelled at by the mate who probably saved lives. Bounce off, enter the lock and with bits of piling embedded in the leeboard head for the inner gates at high speed with no method of stopping. The mate yells "take our line" as we approach ENA, now moored safely, her skipper Brian Pinner (probably a cricketer) makes a deft catch and several tons of oak screeches to a halt with no further damage to any other vessel. Most of the crew is so shocked they are unable to move for several minutes.

"Crew are left wondering where the 'lot of help' mentioned by Flag earlier, was – certainly not present at the moment of crisis.

"Flag demanded the remainder of the fleet enter in an orderly fashion. Conditions are worsening, with wind howling round and round the lock. LAMOUETTE reports engine overheating, stops engine, lifeboat called to assist. WHITE MARLIN ahead of fleet with very sick passenger. Boats are every which way. TRENCHARD has no steering. Dover lifeboat comes in with GENTLE LADY alongside. Someone is playing bagpipes on the lock. Not until midnight, towed gently by tug ATTENTIVE did we make our way through the lock system to tie up in the inner harbour."

In shops all over town there are photographs of soldiers, civilians, buildings in ruins, a town all but annihilated. The photographs depict a terrible scene.

Dunkirk quickly recovered after the war. The locks and basins were restored to full use, train and ferry services to Dover began again. Only a small stretch of The Mole, once out into the sea almost a mile, remains. The old harbour is sedate now that the new Dunkirk West Ferry terminal is built near to Mardyck, occupied by the enemy in 1940, enabling them to fire at will at the beaches, the sea and the vessels attempting to rescue the men trapped there.

Trying to explain in French only that two men sailed a barge in the old days, is good fun. *'Ah non' Dieu! Oui! Sacre Bleu!*

Val is disgusted with the British education system which did not teach her to say:

"I require some heavy duty oil for my gear change mechanism", in her French lessons.

Barbara:

"We entertained to breakfast the three man crew of the LADY HAIG, having found them in their sleeping bags on the quayside. A bit of their open rowing boat broke on the way across so one of them had been home to England to cut down an oak tree and make another bit. (Perhaps he didn't trust French trees.) They had been up all night fixing it so they could join the flotilla. They had a small outboard to help. No – I didn't believe the story either, and I saw them and talked to them. One of them was well over 70 years old. They were the oddest looking bunch, and I am proud to have met them."

Inner Harbour, Dunkirk *

Our engine still has to be re-assembled, although Fritz, an ex-submariner has obtained a gear-change mechanism from HMS *ALACRITY*.

The mate went back to *ALACRITY* next day and was forced to spend a long time in the ward room and became not very well.

PM: The engine finally re-starts. Acknowledgements are due to the navy, Bob, skipper of *BLUEBIRD II*, and an un-named Frenchman. The latter was walking with his family on the quayside, asked what the problem was. He stepped aboard and spent two hours giving advice to skipper whilst working with him on the Kelvin engine. He is an engineer and knows Kelvins well, as there are several working in Dunkirk. His wife and children sat, waiting patiently. He went away and came back with three huge cans of engine oil. Val offered him a drink, which he refused.

"How can we thank you?" she said.

He replied:

"You don't owe me anything. The British took my father off this beach in 1940. We lived a few miles away I was 17 years old, we saw the flames in the sky and heard the bombardment. We thought we would never see him again, but thanks to you he returned. I can never thank YOU".

BBC reporter Kate Aidie working out of the back of a van [*]

By dinner time schoolchildren, English veterans, five French policemen and the Royal Navy are in and out of our saloon all day, all provided with tea and cake.

Sat. 26th May 1990:
Skipper still messing about with his engine, became extraordinarily filthy, got fed up until he was allowed to kiss a French Bride, when he cheered up very much. Crowds of people are on the quay side, telling us more stories. There is a big parade military and veterans. Elderly wives of old men, have tears in their eyes as they murmur *"It is a privilege to be here"*. The flags flutter in the sunshine, the brass band plays, the Little Ships are dressed overall and it is all very pretty.

There is a presentation of commemorative plaques and other mementoes of May 1940 at the Town Hall with lots of speeches from French officials and the British Consul, hands of friendship all round and applause from everyone. Fancy! A dirty old barge being honoured by the French!

Barge wreckage in Dunkirk Museum [*]

Our Skipper, Rob, shook hands with the Captain of HMS *ALCRITY* and began to thank him for all that he had done, but Val quickly intervened, because we are not sure he *knew* all that he had done.

Pilgrims alongside PUDGE in Dunkirk inner harbour *

Sunday 27th May:
Gentle voices in the saloon: Stumbled out to find a French breakfast in progress with someone called Herbie Brown telling more stories. Blokes who had slept on their 'Little Ships' tied alongside us are invited on board. No milk and no shops open. We explain in our best Franglais to a French barkeep lounging in a doorway in his bedroom slippers. He fetched his own milk for us, one of the many kindnesses given and received during these emotional few days. Coaches arrive full of veterans and their wives, who visit the cafes they know, kiss Frenchmen, practice the parade formation. The usual quiet of a Sunday morning in a French seaside town is ruffled, disturbed, broken by the coming of tens, hundreds, thousands who return this day to remember and grieve.

In 1990 an elderly veteran told us:

"We didn't get there until the 3rd June. We were Royal Army Service Corps, coming behind the main force blowing up bridges. We were laying the detonators about three miles away when a troop of French cavalry came across. I later learned that I was only just down the road from where some men from the Norfolk regiment surrendered to Jerry, and they took them into a field and shot them.

"I was out on the Mole later in the evening, picking my way over the dead. Some of those bodies had been there two or three days. Early in the morning the Messerschmitts started on us again, but we couldn't go back. There were hundreds packed on there. We just crouched among the bodies and hoped. If there was a pause we fell asleep. I got onto a cargo boat eventually. No, I couldn't tell you her name. I don't remember the crossing. I was fast asleep".

Another veteran came aboard *PUDGE*:

"With other soldiers I was in a barn, where we were surprised by German soldiers. With some of my mates I jumped into a lorry and we crashed out through a wall, escaping. I learned later that the ones who didn't were taken into a field and shot the next day".

The Le Paradis massacre was a war crime committed by members of the 14th Company, SS Division Totenkopf, under the command of Hauptsturmführer Fritz Knöchlein.

It took place on 27th May 1940, during the Battle of France, at a time when the British troops were attempting to retreat through the Pas-de-Calais region. Soldiers of the 2nd Battalion, the Royal Norfolk Regiment, had become isolated from their regiment. They occupied and defended a farmhouse against an attack by Waffen-SS forces in the village of Le Paradis. It was 17:15, when they ran out of ammunition.

During the battle the Germans attacked the farmhouse with mortars, tanks and artillery shelling, which destroyed the building and forced the defenders to relocate to a cowshed.

After running out of ammunition, the 99 surviving defenders of the 2nd Norfolks were eventually ordered by their commander Major Lisle Ryder, the brother of Robert Edward Dudley Ryder to surrender and they left the cowshed that they had been defending under a white flag.

Due to the boundary between the two British regiments being the road, Ryder's men surrendered not to the company they had been fighting, but rather to SS Hauptsturmführer Fritz Knöchlein's unit, which had been fighting the Royal Scots.

The British captives, a majority of whom were wounded, were disarmed and marched down a road off the Rue du Paradis.

An official account given by Private Albert Pooley, one of the only two survivors:

> *"We turned off the dusty French road, through a gateway and into a meadow beside the buildings of a farm. I saw with one of the nastiest feelings I have ever had in my life two heavy machine guns inside the meadow ... pointing at the head of our column. The guns began to spit fire ... for a few seconds the cries and shrieks of our stricken men drowned the crackling of the guns. Men fell like grass before a scythe ... I felt a searing pain and pitched forward ... my scream of pain mingled with the cries of my mates, but even before I fell into the heap of dying men, the thought stabbed my brain 'If I ever get out of here, the swine that did this will pay for it'".*

Ninety-seven British troops died. Two others survived, with injuries, and hid until they were captured by German forces several days later. Knöchlein then armed his men with bayonets to kill any remaining survivors. Satisfied that they had killed them all, the German soldiers left to rejoin the rest of their regiment.

The Germans forced French civilians to bury the bodies in a shallow mass grave the next day. Despite the German efforts, Private William O'Callaghan had survived and pulled Private Albert Pooley alive from among the bodies in the field.

The pair then hid in a pig-sty for three days and nights, surviving on raw potatoes and water from puddles before being discovered by the farm's owner, Madame Duquenne-Creton, and her son Victor. The French civilians risked their lives caring for the two men, who were later captured by the Wehrmacht's 251st Infantry Division. Mass graves found near Le Paradis in 2007 suggest that around 20 men of the Royal Scots who surrendered to an SS unit may also have been murdered in a separate massacre.

The barn at Le Paradis

After the war, Fritz Knöchlein was located, tried and convicted by a war crimes court, with the two survivors acting as witnesses against him. For his part in the massacre, Knöchlein was executed in 1949.

Record their names with pride *

The parade comes by, including members of the British Legion, accompanied by a British bobby. We hear the command, sotto voce: *"Bags o' swank boys, we're British"*.

And bags of swank they gave us, marching like the young men they once were. A cheer goes up around us.

We stand at the Cenotaph as the wreath is laid there, the flags dipped before rushing back to our boat waved on by the French engineer and his family and several crew from *ALACRITY*.

Bob went to the nearest cemetery:
> "The war graves commission seem to have given the relatives a selection of wording to choose from as there is little variation. Nevertheless it seems the relations did have some say. It did give me a lump in the throat".

A very old man perched on a shooting stick to watch the veteran's parade had brought the widow of one of his men with him.

"I have my husband's ashes in my handbag. He wanted to see this day but he died two months ago. He so wanted to be here so I've brought his ashes, here in my handbag. We shall put them on the beach this afternoon during the memorial service. It's where he left his friends".

A celebratory moment! *

Our crew feeling like Royalty on Dunkirk Town Hall balcony *

In the saloon on PUDGE *

The East Mole, 1990 *

At 14.00 hrs on Sunday we began the last leg of our pilgrimage as the 70 Little Ships that made it out of the 78 that had set out sailed out of the harbour past the East Mole, still lying holed and wounded, a sombre monument to the men who died there and lie in the waters around.

Escorted by the Navy, Army and RAF, approximately 70 Little Ships gently sail or motor a wide circle around an imaginary cross in the water. A helicopter flew in and dropped a wreath in the centre of our formation, all ships dipped their ensigns and 7,000 veterans and their families and friends on shore saluted. The Battle of Britain flight flew past, followed by the Red Arrows streaming red white and blue smoke, a fitting reminder that we grasped victory out of defeat.

The crew of *PUDGE* has a wreath of Poppies from Deptford British Legion, a wreath from the Thames Barge Sailing Club, two posies of cornflowers and a very old Union Jack to lay off the beach from a lady who never gave her name, but brought them to us in Dover.

As we laid our tributes on the water, a mark of respect for the men that died here Bob speaks for us:

"We have returned today to remember all those who gave their lives during the nine days of Operation Dynamo, 50 years ago. We remember especially John Edward Atkins, third hand on the barge LADY ROSEBERY. On behalf of his family we place these wreaths near the spot where John was killed. We do this as a mark of respect for him and all like him who have no known grave."

And because we have no words that seem good enough we use those of Laurence Binyon:
> *"They shall not grow old as we that our left grow old.*
> *Age shall not weary them nor the years condemn.*
> *At the going down of the sun and in the morning*
> *We shall remember them"*

Each of us has our own memories. For Val it was the Frenchman who brought the oil. For Tony the wreath laying, for Bob the war cemetery, for Simon the people who wanted to share their memories. For them I tried to write as much down as I could so as not to let the experience be forgotten.

Opposite us at the reception on board *WAVERLY,* upon our return to England sat a young German woman:
> *"We do not grieve like this. We do not have special occasions like this when we can remember our dead with pride and honour. Yet they believed they were fighting for a just cause, for their families, for the fatherland. Even now, when I travel around Europe I sometimes see the look in people's eyes when I say I am German and I know they resent me. It is important to be able to remember, to grieve, to have pride in yourself or you stay angry and it is all inside. My father never speaks of these things and he becomes angry if you ask him. If we do not remember how bad it was for us all perhaps it could happen again."*

31ˢᵗ MAY 1940

John Atkins, born in Kent, 1925, wrote a letter home.

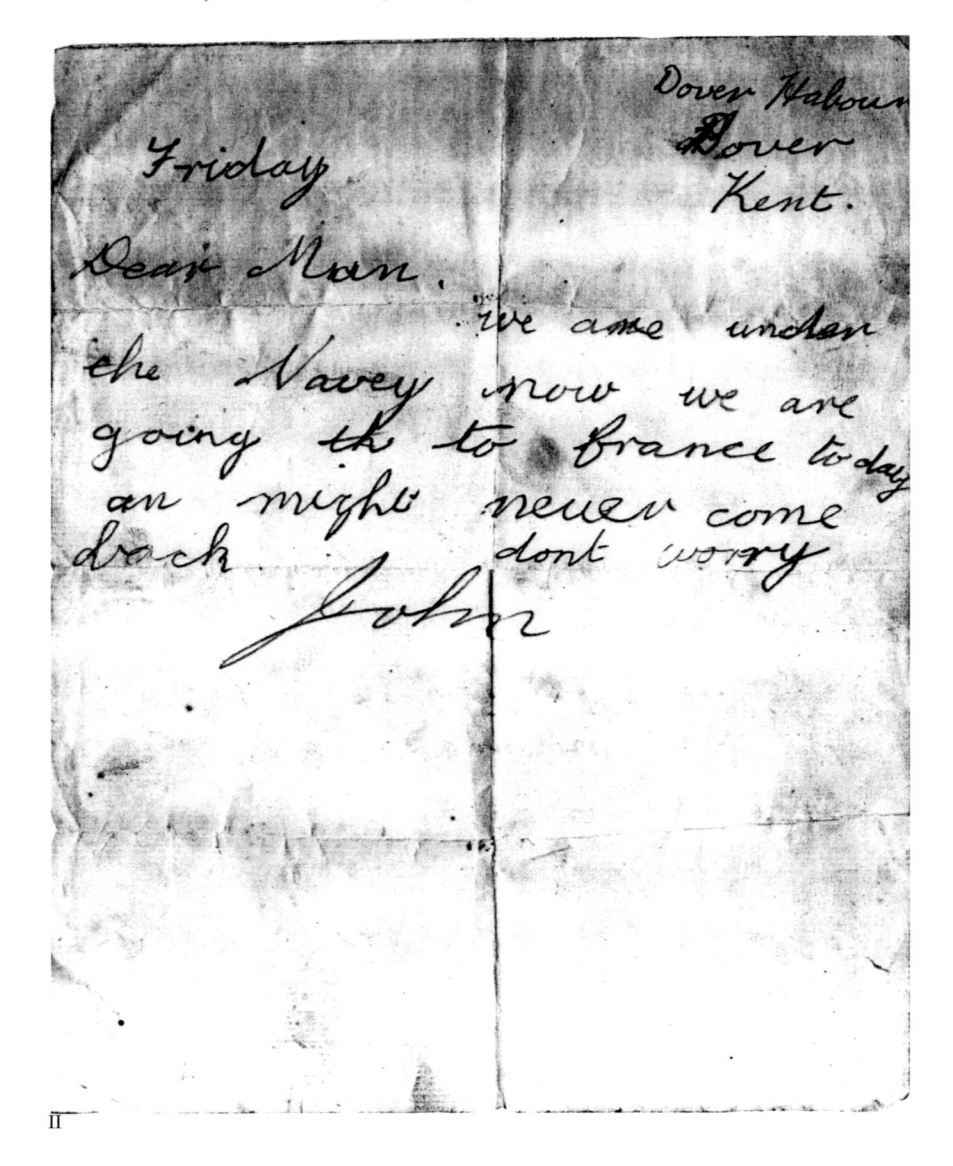

> Dover Habour
> Dover
> Kent.
>
> Friday
>
> Dear Mum,
>
> we ame unden the Navey now we are going th to france today an might never come back dont worry
>
> John

John Atkins [II]

John was the cook/third hand on the *LADY ROSEBERY*. Together with *DORIS* and *PUDGE* she sailed to Dunkirk on the 31st May 1940. The tug that was towing them, *ST. FAGAN,* hit a mine and sank. Only *PUDGE* survived the explosion. John went down with *LADY ROSEBERY.*

He did not have a coming home parade. His family did not see his coffin covered in the British flag. He lies at the bottom of the cold sea off the beach at Dunkirk, beside the East Mole.

But on the 31st May 1940 he was a hero who gave his life to try to save his fellow countrymen. He was 15 years old.

THE END

APPENDIX 1

TROOPS EVACUATED

Date	Troops evacuated from beaches	Troops evacuated from Dunkirk Harbour	Total
Mon 27 May	-	7,669	7,669
Tues 28 May	5,930	11,874	17,804
Wed 29 May	13,752	33,558	47,310
Thurs 30 May	29,512	24,311	53,823
Fri 31 May	22,942	45,072	68,014
Sat 1 June	17,348	47,081	64,429
Sun 2 June	6,695	19,561	26,256
Mon 3 June	1,870	24,876	26,746
Tues 4 June	622	25,553	26,175
Totals	98,671	239,555	338,226

APPENDIX 2.

ASSOCIATION OF DUNKIRK LITTLE SHIPS

Qualification for full membership is to be the current owner of a proven Dunkirk Little Ship. The object of the Association is equally simple: to keep afloat for as long as possible as many as possible of the original Little Ships; to secure for them the honour to which they are entitled; and thereby to preserve "The Spirit of Dunkirk".

The term Little Ship applies to all craft that were originally privately owned and includes commercial vessels such as barges, British, French, Belgian and Dutch fishing vessels and pleasure steamers. The Association does include some ex-Service vessels, which are now privately owned, and ex-Lifeboats.

The Cross of St.George (the flag of Admiralty) defaced with the Arms of Dunkirk is the Association's House Flag. This can be worn by Member Ships at any time when the owner is aboard. In addition, when in company, the un-defaced Cross of St. George at the bow may be flown, by Admiralty Warrant. To avoid any possible confusion with barges wearing an Admiral's flag, the Dunkirk Little Ships must wear the Red Ensign when flying the un-defaced Flag of St. George at the bows.

Wherever a member ship is seen, this proud emblem is now recognised.

You can buy a Lordship of the Manor, even, it is rumoured a seat in the House of Lords, but you cannot buy the right to fly the flag of the Association of Little Ships. It is reserved for the vessels that were there. Not the owners, past or present, but the boat herself.

Sailing Barges that are Members of the Association of Dunkirk Little Ships:

BEATRICE MAUD
CABBY
DAWN
ENA
ETHEL MAUD
GLENWAY
GRETA
NANCIBELLE
PUDGE
TOLLESBURY
VIKING

APPENDIX 3

French site: Epaves a Dunkerque: dkepaves.free.fr includes vessels sunk during Operation Dynamo, marked with OD. The site contains inaccuracies.

OD 151 s.b Ada Mary
OD 151 a.b Advance
OD 151 s.b.Aidie
OD 151 s.b Barbara Jean
OD 151 s.b Basildon
OD 151 s.b Beatrice Maud
OD 151 s.b Burton
OD 152 a.b Cabby
OD 152 d.b Charlotte
OD 152 s.b Claude
OD 152 d.b's.D1, D16, D4, D7, D9. Owner Silvertown Services
OD 153 dumb barges FW 23 & Kitty
OD 152 s.b Dawn
OD 152 s.b Duchess
OD 153 s.b Ena
OD 153 s.b Ethel Everard
OD 153 s.b Ethel Maud
OD 153 s.b Glenway
OD 153 s.b Greta
OD 153 s.b H.A.C.
OD 153 s.b Haste Away
OD 153 s.b Lady Richmond probably Lucy Richmond
OD 153 s.b Lady Rosemary? Probably Lady Rosebery
OD 153 s.b Lark
OD 153 barge Mary
OD 154 a.b Mousma
OD 154 a.b Plinlimmon
OD 154 a.b Pudge
OD 154 s.b Queen
OD 154 s.b Queen Alexandra, owner Turmaine and Jones
OD 154 s.b Royalty

OD 154 d.b Sark
OD 154 a.b Seine
OD 154 s.b Shannon
OD 154 a.b Sherfield
OD 154 d.b Shetland
OD 154 s.b Spurgeon
OD 154 d.b Surrey
OD 154 a.b Thyra
OD 154 s.b Tollesbury
OD 154 s.b Unique
OD 154 a.b Viking
OD 154 s.b Warrior
OD 154 s.b Westall

APPENDIX 4

Essex Family History Barges at War, Operation Dynamo:

Barges that survived post O.D	Barges that were lost
ADA MARY	*AIDEE*
BEATRICE MAUD	*BURTON*
CABBY	*BARBARA JEAN*
ENA	*CLAUDE*
GLENWAY	*DORIS*
H.A.C.	*DUCHESS*
HASTE AWAY	*ETHEL EVERARD*
LADY SHEILA	*LADY ROSEBERY*
MONARCH	*LARK*
PUDGE	*QUEEN*
QUEEN ALEXANDRA	*ROYALTY*
SEINE	*VALONIA*
SHANNON	*WARRIOR*
SHERFIELD	
SPURGEON	
THYRA	
TOLLESBURY	
VIKING	

INDEX OF BARGES MENTIONED HEREIN

Page:-

ADA MARY	128, 140, 141, 143, 232
AIDIE, (ADIE AIDEE)	70, 87, 99, 107, 113, 133, 136, 232, 234
ADVANCE	170, 232
ALDERMAN	189, 191
AILSA	188
ALARIC	189
ASHINGTON	168, 169
AUDREY	87, 94
BARBARA JEAN	70, 86, 92, 94, 99, 107, 113, 114, 133, 136, 137, 138, 232, 234
BANKSIDE	189, 190
BASILDON	168, 169, 232
BEATRICE MAUD	71, 72, 73, 76, 82, 99, 160, 231, 232, 234
BIJOU	94, 190 *also named GRAVELINES II, page 190*
BURTON	128, 141, 142, 143, 232, 234
CABBY	1, 170, 210, 212, 231, 232, 234
CASTANET	189
CENTAUR	140, 171
CLAUDE	29, 232, 234
CHARLOTTE	232 no other information
DAWN	135, 231, 232
DORIS	47, 50, 56, 71, 91, 107, 113, 133, 228, 234
DUCHESS	49, 71, 102, 105, 133, 135, 232, 234
DULUTH	187
EDME	190
ENA	1, 4, 49, 88, 91, 94, 107, 120, 146, 155, 158, 161, 209, 212, 231, 231, 234
ENCHANTRESS	189
ETHEL MAUD	97, 231, 232
ETHEL EVERARD	70, 199, 108, 115, 116, 117, 133, 232, 234
WILL EVERARD, FRED EVERARD, ALF EVERARD	115
GENERAL JACKSON	189
GLENWAY	71, 83, 118, 138, 162, 231, 232, 234
GLENDIVO, GLENMOVE, GLENBURN, GLENCOE, GLENBURY	119
GOLDEVE	29, 30

GOLDBELL, GOLDCROWN, GOLDRIFT,	30
GRAVELINES	94
GRETA	84, 188, 231, 232
H.A.C. (INVICTA)	49, 73, 82, 147, 160, 232, 234
HASTE AWAY	189, 140, 143, 232, 234
HERBERT	189
HILDA	190
H.K.D.	187
JOCK	94, 158
KINGFISHER	189
KNOWLES	189
LADY DAPHNE	158
LADY JEAN	94
LADY SHEILA	234
LADY ROSEBERY (LADY ROSEMARY)	42, 47, 57, 71, 133, 225, 228, 232, 234
LARK	71, 83, 118, 133, 138, 140, 171, 232, 234
LUCY RICHMOND (LADY RICHMOND)	78, 79, 232
MARIE MAY	145
MARY, may refer to either ADA MARY or MARIE MAY	232
MAJOR	187
MONARCH	171, 234
MOUSMA (MOUSME)	170, 232
NANCIBELLE	118, 231
ORINOCO	94, 158
PHOENICIAN	75
PLINLIMMON	172, 232
PUDGE	1, 4, 47, 56, 60, 71, 82, 115, 209, 211, 228, 231, 232, 234
QUEEN	172, 232, 234
QUEEN ALEXANDRA	172, 232, 234
RAYBELL	94
RESOLUTE	189
ROYALTY	71, 73, 82, 98, 105, 118, 133, 160, 232, 234
ROSME	190
SARK	99, 118, 233
SEINE	169, 233, 234
SHANNON	128, 142, 233, 234

SHERFIELD	140, 233, 234
SHETLAND	99, 118, 233
SPURGEON	119, 121, 138, 233, 234
THALATTA	94, 158
THOMAS AND FRANCES	187
THYRA	49, 71, 73, 82, 98, 160, 233, 234
TOLLESBURY	5, 49, 70, 91, 99, 107, 116, 157, 231, 233, 234
TRILBY	94
VALONIA	171, 234
VICTOR	114, 188
VIKING	65, 231, 233, 234
WARRIOR	172, 233, 234
WESTALL	136, 233
WHY NOT?	187
WOODHAM COURT	189
WYVENHOE	190

BIBLIOGRAPHY

Contributions acknowledged:

David and Elizabeth Wood for Eric Stuart's account, passed on by his widow.
Charlie Webb's Life on Barges passed by him to Richard Smith and on to David.
Keith Webb for Lem Webb's letter dated June 1940 and family photographs.
The Atkins family for John's letter and photograph given to Tony Farnham.

Publications:

The Port of Ipswich, It's Shipping and Trades: Richard W. Smith and Jill Freestone. Malthouse Press, Suffolk, 2011. ISBN 978-0-9539680-4-6

The Thames Barge in Suffolk, Richard W. Smith, Society for Spritsail Barge Research 2006. ISBN 0-9552489-0-6

A Cross in the Topsail, Roger Finch, The Boydell Press, 1979, ISBN 0 85115 113 2.

The Ships That Saved an Army, Russell Plummer, Patrick Stephens Ltd, 1990, ISBN 1-85260-210-4.

The Second World War, Winston Churchill, Cassell, 1949.

Winston Churchill, from the Diaries of Lord Moran, Heron Books, 1966.

CHURCHILL, a biography, Martin Gilbert, Doubleday and Company, Inc., Garden City, New York. 1980 ISBN 0-385-15587-5

The Miracle of Dunkirk by Walter Lord, Wandsworth Editions, 1982, ISBN 1 85326 685 X.

The Epic of Dunkirk, E. Keble Chatterton, Hurst and Blackett Ltd. 1940.

Dunkirk 1940: Wherabouts Unknown, Tim Lynch, Spellmount, The History Press, 2010. ISBN 978 0 7524 5490 0.

A Handbook of Sailing Barges, by F.S. Cooper, Adlard Coles Ltd. of Southampton in asn. George G. Harrap Ltd. London, 1955.

Amateur Sailor, Nicholas Drew, Constable & Co. Ltd. 1944.

The War in Pictures, Odhams Press Ltd. 1946

Sailing Barges, Frank G.G. Carr, Hodder and Stroughton, reprinted 1931.

The Thames and All That – A History of the river by A.G.Thompson, published by The General Steam Navigation Company 1935

The Nine Days of Dunkirk, David Divine, W.W.Norton and Co. Inc. 1959.

Us Bargemen by A.S. Bennett, Meresborough, 1980, ISBN 0 905270 207.

A Conversation with Dick, the Dagger as told to Tony Farnham, Chaffcutter books, 2001, ISBN 0-9532422-6-9.

Epics of the Sea, A.A. Hoehling, Contemporary Books Inc. 1977, ISBN 0-8092-8129-5.

The Evacuation from Dunkirk, Frank Cass, Whitehall History Publishing Consortium, Crown Copyright 2000. (HMSO Copyright Unit.

Thames Barge Sailing Club Journal, Autumn 1992.

Orwell Estuary by W.G. Arnott, published by Norman Allard and Co. 1954

Dover Castle by Jonathan Coad, English Heritage publication, 2011. ISBN 978 1 84802 097 9.

The Thames by D.G.Wilson, A Batsford Book ISBN 07134 52986

Whereabouts Unknown by Tim Lynch, The History Press, 2010. ISBN: 9780752454900

Dunkirk Withdrawal: Operation Dynamo, May 26 to June 1940: Alphabetical List of Vessels Taking Part with Their Services, Compiled by Godfrey Philip Orde

In popular culture:

The Snow Goose, Paul Gallico. 1941.

The Postmistress, Sarah Blake, Berkley Books, 2011, ISBN 978-0-425-23869-1.

Suite Francaise, Irene Nemirovsky, Vintage Books, 2006, ISBN 978-1-4000-9627-5.

We Are at War, Simon Garfield, Ebury Press, 2006, ISBN 9780091903879.

The Guernsey Literary and Potato Peel Pie Society, Mary Ann Shaffer and Annie Barrows, Bloomsbury Press, 2008, ISBN 978 1 4088 1026 2.

Atonement, Ian McEwan, Vintage at Random House, 2002, ISBN 0 09 942979 9

<u>Societies and websites of interest:</u>

Association of Dunkirk Little Ships: www.adls.org.uk

Society for Sailing Barge Research: John White, Hon Secretary, 5 Cox Road, Alresford, Colchester, Essex CO7 8EJ including:-
George Faint Archives, Frank Willmott Archives sourced from website of SSBR, Data transcribed from handwritten ledgers.
Peter Josh in SSBR Magazine 'Mainsheet' No 93.
Topsail, various The Journals of the Society for Spritsail Barge Research including *Dunkirk Relived by Arthur Joscelyne published by SSBR Topsail magazine No. 23, 1987.* Also Mainsheet, the Society Magazine.

Waldringfield History Group: www.waldringfieldia.com

French site: Epaves a Dunkerque: www.dkepaves.free.fr : This site includes all the documents gathered over the years on sunken wrecks off Dunkirk. There are inaccuracies.

Essex Family History: The Bargemen and The Thames Barge at war - historical information on spritsail barges by name. It gives 30 sailing/auxilliary barges involved in Operation Dynamo. www.essex-family-history.co.uk

www.bargemen.co.uk : History and photographs on Thames Barges that played a part in "Operation Dynamo", the evacuation from Dunkirk in 1940.

The web site of the steam tug Challenge www.stchallenge.org

www.thamestugs.co.uk   THAMES TUGS for Logs of tugs at Dunkirk. Incomplete list.

dalyhistory.wordpress.com/2010/02/13/trawlers-drifters-and-tugs

uk.groups.yahoo.com/group/Thames_Barges

http://merseamuseum.org.uk/mmbarges.php
The entries from the Mercantile Navy list for 1938 have been extracted from the Mersea Museum website. Entries on this site had been copied several times and mistakes may have crept in for which the Mersea Museum and this author take no responsibility.

Commonealth War Graves Commission.

Forces war records at www.qaranc.co.uk

'A Very Ordinary Place' by Barbara Butler, published by the author.

INDEX OF ATTRIBUTIONS FOR ILLUSTRATIONS

Owned or photographed by the author   *

'Winston Churchill' – Moran   1

'The War in Pictures'   2

www.bargemen.co.uk   3

dkepaves.free.fr   4

Andrew Berry, TSBT.   5

www.thames tugs.co.uk   6

Society for Sailing Barge Research   7

The Webb family   8

'A Cross in the Topsail'   9

'The Thames'   10

Tony Farnham, SSBR   11

luisphoto@bibtelecom.net (Gibraltar)   +

s.b. BEATRICE MAUD – additional information.

Past editor of the Thames Barge Sailing Club Journals, Elizabeth Wood, has contributed an article from winter 1956. Sully's, owners of this barge reported a visit to their office of a brother of French officer Lt. Jose Heron, who with other French soldiers rescued (or were rescued by!) *BEATRICE MAUD*. He gave them a copy of Lt. Heron's account:

"About midnight on the 3rd June 1940, the French and British Admiralties ordered that the evacuation of troops should cease leaving near forty thousand men still on the beaches of Malo-les-Bains. About 4 am on the 4th Heron reached the shore with a small detachment of men from the rearguard. The Germans were occupying Dunkirk, the remaining allied troops caught like rats in a narrow trap, had no chance to escape except by sea. At dawn the pale calm sea only offered a misty horizon with wrecks of many ships sunk during the evacuation standing out like skeletons.

"The first German tanks and armoured cars could be heard approaching along the lanes leading to the Malo les Bains. Men were, hoping to find some boat that would still float. We found several holed boats but finally, about a mile from Dunkirk East Pier I came across a small fishing boat full of water. One of the men pointed out that she was unseaworthy, being full of water. We bailed her out and found two good oars under the thwarts. With some difficulty we got her down the 200 yards to the sea. Nine of us got aboard, and as the boat had only five or six inches of freeboard had to row very carefully. I decided to make for a torpedo boat which although listing from a distance appeared seaworthy, only 400 yards offshore. Alas! We found that she was a complete wreck with not a living soul on board.

"I was worried though about attempting a crossing to England in an open boat, only 14 feet long with nine men on board. We had little chance of making a safe crossing, and several of the men were fathers of families. Then, through the

morning mist, I caught sight on a boat fitted with leeboards drifting southwards with the current. At first I took her to be a small fishing boat, but gradually, as we drew alongside, I saw that she was a big Thames barge. The outline was familiar to me as I have often seen pictures of these craft.

"I tried to attract the barge's attention with my signalling lamp from about 200 yards, but there was no sign on life on board. We came alongside and some French soldiers popped up from the hold. Scrambling on deck we found that we were on the barge Beatrice Maud of London; she already had about 250 French soldiers on board. They had come onboard the day before, 3rd June at Malo-Les-Baines, They had waited eight days and nights on the beach for evacuation, under incessant bombing, Absolutely exhausted, these men boarded the barge. They thought they would be safer a sea than on land, even though they had no idea where they were going.

I took charge of the Beatrice Maud, as I was the only one on board with any knowledge of sailing I found an acrobat and an ex marine amongst the men, and with this 'crew' managed to hoist the sails and lower the leeboards. As we were getting about the German tanks were penetrating onto the beaches running up and down rounding up any troops that were left. We had incredible luck in being able to reach the barge just half an hour before the Germans arrived. I still tremble to think that if these providential circumstances had not occurred, we would have had to face five years of captivity in Germany.

"As soon as the sails were hoisted I took the helm. I felt quite proud to command this fine craft, and to feel her gliding along in the gentle breeze. Alas, after less than a quarter of an hour, we were carried between two grounded cargo boats only 100 yards apart and the Beatrice Maud was ashore on a sandbank. It was low tide; the men on board were so exhausted that none of them noticed we were aground and we refloated about half an hour later.

"A mist surrounded the sea, blotting out the coastline, hiding us completely from the eyes of the Germans. I am certain that this saved us. Without this friendly mist the Germans certainly would not have forgotten us.

"As soon as we refloated, I took the helm and set course approximately North West in the hope of reaching Dover or Folkestone. We sailed all morning with a gentle breeze from the North North West. Every now and then we passed through a graveyard of wrecks, cases and drifting boats.

"About midday the wind began to freshen, causing a slight swell. Several times during the morning we picked up men from overloaded rowing boats attempting the crossing. These frail craft would certainly have been in trouble in the high seas we met later on. We sailed on through the afternoon in a freshening wind About 3pm I had to get the topsail down using only the foresail, mainsail and mizzen.

"I began to feel very tired about 5pm as I had not left the wheel since early morning. I gave the wheel to a companion to whom I had given a little instruction in the art of sailing and went below. I had not been lying down a quarter of an hour when I was called on deck because of broken water dead ahead. We were heading straight for a sandbank. I immediately turned about and sailed back on our track for an hour or so then steered South West. After another hour I steered North North West again near a half submerged lightship, absolutely deserted. It was very difficult to distinguish the name in the poor visibility perhaps it was the South Goodwin.

"We were now spinning along at a good speed, when about 7pm the lookout in the bow reported that he could see something through the fog. Through my binoculars I saw the outline of a small naval craft, then a second, then a third. They proved to be armed trawlers.

"We headed towards one of them and passing close under her bow I hoisted the letter "T" flag of the international code, the reverse side of which shows, blue, white and red and asked her name and the direction of the nearest port; the reply came from the bridge 'Dover, just a mile'.

"Soon the fog lifted and we saw the cliffs of Dover, God be praised! Because of the difficulty of entering harbour under sail with so poor a crew I decided to ask the trawler to tow us in. We were drifting southwards, so I dropped anchor and furled the sails. The sea was rough now, and the trawler was circling us waiting for the right moment to take us in tow.

"We waited about a quarter of an hour and finally the trawler put a man on board to assist us. W tried to weigh anchor, but the rough sea made this an impossible operation, so we sawed through the chain and slipped the anchor. The trawler then took us in tow but the rope broke twice. We then threw them one of our own ropes that we had found neatly coiled up in the bow. This held us and we entered Dover Harbour at 8pm.

A large crowd gathered on the quay as we came ashore. It was low tide so ladders had to be provided so that we could climb up on the quay. We were well received by the British particularly the Red Cross who supplied us with all kinds of things. I remember those small delicious English sausages. Having starved for so many days I devoured a great number, I do not think that many Englishmen believed our story to be strictly true, perhaps because it has been only on rare occasions during the past centuries that the French have returned an English ship to England.

"I would have been very pleased to have met the owner of Beatrice Maud and hand his ship back to him personally after crossing from Dunkirk to Dover with more than 300 soldiers on board. The same night we were sent to a reception camp at Southampton. On 6th June we were repatriated, sailing in the steamer Vienna to Cherbourg. The battle of France was not yet over. My family and I are deeply grateful to God for allowing me, with so many of my comrades to escape the misery of five years captivity. In memory of this marvellous epic, one of my daughters has been named Beatrice Maud".